BUILDING THE BEST TRUST

A HANDY GUIDE
TO PROTECT ASSETS,
REDUCE TAXES, AVOID COSTLY
MISTAKES, AND TRANSFER
GENERATIONAL WEALTH
TO YOUR HEIRS

BENJAMIN CARTER

Read and Learn Publishing™
Promised Harbour Publications
Buffalo, Wyoming

ISBN-10: 0999745255
ISBN-13: 978-0-9997452-5-0
Library of Congress Control Number: 2025901837
Printed in the United States of America

Chapter Table of Contents

Section Table of Contents

INTRODUCTION

Do you possibly have friends who believe their estate planning is complete? They have respectable savings and investments, a family home, and cherished heirlooms. They may have mentioned the fact they have a will, and have asked a close trusted friend who is an attorney to step in and act as Executor to make sure their will is faithfully probated. The problem is, a will may not be enough.

Family members going through the trauma of losing a loved one are vulnerable. Even when decedents have made careful provisions in their will, survivors now have to go through the probate process. Did you know that probate takes all your plans for passing on your estate to your heirs and puts them on public legal display – out of your control – and theirs? There is a much better way.

We are talking about a Trust. You can set up a Trust for your family. This book will show you how. Keep reading and see for yourself how a Trust done right will give you the power to protect your assets, reduce taxes, avoid costly mistakes, and secure your financial legacy. Whether you're planning for your family's future or just starting to explore your options, this book provides the guidance you need.

Learn how to build the best Trust – the one that is right for you now – while you still live – and right for those who will inherit your estate.

Trusts are more than just legal documents. They are powerful tools designed to protect what you've worked hard to build. They help you manage your wealth, ensure your wishes are honored, and provide for your loved ones. Trusts offer benefits like asset protection, tax efficiency, and flexible wealth transfer. They are tailored to fit your unique circum- stances and goals.

In today's financial landscape, trusts have become increasingly relevant. Family dynamics can be complex, and legal costs are rising. Personalized estate planning solutions are in high demand, and trusts offer exactly that. They provide a way to navigate these challenges and offer peace of mind knowing that your assets are managed according to your wishes.

This book is meant for any prospective party to a trust, especially potential grantors. If you are considering setting up a trust or just want to understand how trusts can benefit you and your family, this book was written with you in mind. As you read, you will discover hidden jewels of information that may fill in possible knowledge gaps. You will also hear certain concepts repeated throughout this narrative intended to guide you in your preparation to start building your best trust.

We begin by defining a trust and why it matters. You will learn the different types of trusts and how to choose the right one for your needs. As you read, you will discover the legal framework of trusts and the importance of finding the right attorney. You will get a feel for what it means to be a trustee and learn how to fund your trust. Tax implications and strategies for equitable distribution are among the many topics covered as well as strategies for protecting your assets from creditors, and – even a special trust for entrepreneurs.

Are you ready to take control of your financial future?

Looking for a friend to walk with you on this journey?

This book, "BUILDING THE BEST TRUST" seeks to build a bond of trust with you as you begin to make plans for managing your estate. This book is your new friend.

Through its pages, you can explore trust management responsibilities and points to consider when you choose your trustee. Throughout each chapter, you'll find practical advice and actionable steps. As you read this book, it will equip you with knowledge and confidence to find the additional help and facts you will need to make an informed decisions about your estate planning.

The key takeaway from this book is empowerment.

Knowledge is power. The knowledge you will gain from these pages will help you start the process and put things in motion that will protect your assets, reduce taxes, and ensure a smooth transfer of wealth to your heirs.

CHAPTER 1
UNDERSTANDING TRUSTS

Consider the meticulous couple who believed their estate planning was in good order. They had a house, adequate savings, and a will. They never considered establishing a trust.

When a friend suggested they should at least look into it, they said they would think about it but to be honest, they felt a trust was only for the rich and famous. It was certainly too costly and complicated for them. Time passed and, in time, so did they, believing they had carefully provided for their children. Unfortunately, their children went through months of probate, unexpected taxes, and legal battles.

Isolated example? Hardly. This story could be repeated over and over again. Too many hardworking, honest, well- meaning estate owners misunderstand the purpose, power, and scope of a Trust. They get scared away by the fear of a costly complicated process and never take the time to simply learn the facts.

Trusts can simplify your estate planning, protect your assets, and provide peace of mind. Let's explore what a trust is, how it works, and why it might be the key to securing your financial future.

1.1 WHAT IS A TRUST

To put it simply, a Trust is a contract – a legal agreement between three parties: the Grantor, the Trustee, and the Beneficiary. The grantor transfers assets to the trustee for the benefit the beneficiary. This is a trust agreement, a contract detailing how assets should be managed and distributed. The grantor is the person who creates the trust and transfers assets into it. The trustee follows the instructions of the grantor, holds and manages the assets the grantor transferred to the trust – acting in the best interest of the beneficiaries. A beneficiary is a person or some other recognized corporate entity benefits from who receives income or assets as legally stipulated in the trust document. A trust provides legal authority and flexibility to manage and control assets during the Grantor's lifetime and beyond.

Trusts serve various purposes but are primarily used for asset protection, estate planning, and ensuring privacy. They shield your assets from creditors and potential legal challenges, which can be crucial if you're in a profession with high liability risks. Trusts are a cornerstone of estate planning, allowing for the smooth and efficient transfer of wealth to your heirs without the need for probate, which can be a lengthy and public process. They also maintain privacy by keeping your financial affairs out of public records. This is particularly important for those who value discretion or have complex family situations. By providing specific instructions on how and when assets should be distributed, trusts can help alleviate family disputes and ensure that your wishes are honored.

The structure of a trust is built around specific key components: the trust corpus, fiduciary responsibility, and distribution terms. The trust corpus refers to assets placed into the trust. These include real estate, investments, cash, or other valuables. The trustee executes fiduciary responsibility. He or she is legally obligated to act in the best interest of the beneficiaries. This includes managing the trust's assets prudently, keeping detailed records, and communicating with beneficiaries about the trust's status and distributions. Distribution terms specify how and when the beneficiaries will receive their portion of the trust. This can be adapted many different ways to meet needs and goals. This could mean providing regular income, making one-time lump-sum payments, or setting conditions that must be met before distributions occur.

In this book, we want to walk together on a discovery of the facts and melt away the cobwebs of commonly held misconceptions and false assumptions. One common myth is that trusts are only for the wealthy. In reality, trusts can benefit individuals of all income levels, offering asset protection and estate planning advantages that are valuable regardless of wealth. Another misconception; trusts are too complex or expensive. While it's true that creating a trust involves some initial costs and legal work, these are often outweighed by the long-term benefits provided, such as avoiding probate and reducing taxes. Many also believe that setting up a trust means losing control of assets; however, if they understood how a revocable trust works, they would see how the Grantor retains significant control during his or her lifetime.

Trusts are powerful versatile legal tools that can be tailored to unique specific situations while protecting assets and meeting real needs. Through the power of a trust, you can guarantee critical financial support for loved ones or make sure donations continue to flow to charitable causes.

Before you build your Best Trust, you must understand what a trust is and how it functions. Only then will you be able to make an informed decision about whether a trust is the right tool for you. By dispelling common myths and highlighting the tangible benefits, you can see how trusts offer a practical solution to many estate planning challenges. This chapter lays the foundation for exploring the different types of trusts and how they can be tailored to fit your unique needs and goals.

1.2 TRUSTS vs WILLS: KEY DIFFERENCES AND BENEFITS

The distinction between a trust and a will is important.

A will is a legal document that outlines how you wish your assets to be distributed upon your death. It goes into effect only after you pass away. Any assets governed by a will typically must go through probate. Probate is a court-supervised process. They authenticate the will and distribute your assets. This process can be lengthy and public, exposing your financial affairs to anyone who might be interested.

A trust lets you manage your assets during your lifetime and after your death. A trust can bypass the probate process entirely. This not only ensures a more private handling of your affairs but provides immediate asset distribution. Urgent financial needs are not put on hold.

A trust offers significant privacy advantages. When a will goes through probate, it becomes a public record, revealing the details of your estate to the public. A trust usually avoids probate, keeping your financial matters private. Confidential matters pertaining to your estate are shared only among the involved parties.

Additionally, trusts provide flexibility in asset distribution. They allow you to set the terms that govern when and how your beneficiaries receive their inheritance. Whether you wish to stagger distributions over time or set conditions that must be met, trusts offer you the ability to tailor these aspects to suit your family's needs and circumstances.

Despite their differences, trusts and wills can work together seamlessly in estate planning.

A testamentary trust, for instance, is a type of trust that is created through a will and comes into effect upon your passing. This can be particularly useful if you want to leave assets to minor children or set aside funds for specific purposes that require delayed distribution. A will and a trust may supplement each other to your advantage.

When you have assets that must go through probate or if you wish to outline specific guardianship provisions for minor children, you may combine a will with a trust to ensure all aspects of your estate are covered, providing comprehensive protection and clarity for your heirs.

Trusts hold several advantages over wills in specific scenarios. If you were to become incapacitated, a trust allows for the immediate management of your assets without court intervention. This can be vital for maintaining financial stability and covering medical expenses. For families with minor children or special needs beneficiaries, trusts enable you to set up specific provisions that ensure their care and financial support, which a will alone cannot provide as effectively. Trusts can manage and protect assets without waiting for the probate process, making them more efficient in addressing immediate needs.

Wills, on the other hand, come with limitations that trusts can overcome. The public nature of probate can lead to potential disputes, as family members or other interested parties may contest the will. Once a will is executed, you lose control over the assets.

Trusts, particularly revocable ones, allow you to retain control and make changes as needed during your lifetime. This adaptability can be invaluable in adjusting to changing family circumstances or financial situations. Trusts also provide a level of financial security and management that wills cannot match, ensuring that your wishes are honored both in life and after death.

1.3 COMMON TRUST TYPES EXPLAINED

Let us first consider the difference between Revocable and Irrevocable trusts.

Each trust structure is a foundational choice, offering unique attributes. A Revocable Trust, allows the Grantor to alter or dissolve the trust during his or her lifetime. This flexibility is ideal for those who anticipate changes in their circumstances or preferences. It provides ease in estate planning without immediate tax implications because the assets remain part of the Grantor's estate for tax purposes.

On the other hand, an Irrevocable trust, once established,

cannot be modified or terminated without the Beneficiary's consent. This permanence offers advantages such as asset protection from creditors and potential tax benefits, as assets placed in an irrevocable trust are usually no longer part of the taxable estate. Choosing between these two different trust strategies depends on what the Grantor wants – control versus financial protection and tax planning.

Two addition trust structures further expand the options available to you, the Grantor: Living Trusts and Testamentary Trusts. A living trust, also known as an "inter vivos" trust, comes into play during the grantor's lifetime, allowing for continued asset management and probate avoidance. This trust offers a seamless transition of asset management if the grantor becomes incapacitated, ensuring financial matters are handled according to their wishes without court intervention. On the other hand, a will can establish a testamentary trust that only takes effect upon the grantor's death. It serves effectively for post-death asset distribution, particularly when the grantor wishes to provide for minor children or establish specific conditions for inheritance. Each type of trust serves distinct purposes. Individuals tailor estate planning to fit their specific needs and life situations.

A special needs trusts will become vital for families with dependents requiring special care. These trusts are crafted to provide for dependents with disabilities without compromising their eligibility for government assistance programs like Medicaid or Supplemental Security Income (SSI). This is crucial because receiving an inheritance directly could disqualify them from these benefits. A special needs trust manages the assets in a way that supplements government support, offering tailored asset management to address the dependent's unique needs, from healthcare to personal expenses. This type of trust ensures that the dependent's quality of life is maintained without losing essential public benefits.

Charitable trusts present yet another avenue, blending philanthropy with financial planning. These trusts allow individuals to support charitable causes while enjoying tax advantages. Charitable remainder trusts, for example, provide income to the grantor or beneficiaries for a specified period. Once the period expires, any remaining assets are donated to charity. This structure not only supports philanthropic goals but also offers benefits like avoiding capital gains tax on appreciated assets and providing a current-year income tax deduction. Charitable lead trusts, in contrast, first pay income to a designated charity for a set term, after which the remaining assets revert to the grantor's heirs. This approach can effectively reduce estate taxes while fulfilling charitable intentions.

Understanding these trust types equips you with the knowledge to make informed decisions about estate planning, considering both personal and financial goals. This chapter highlights how the right trust can cater to diverse needs, whether it's maintaining control over your assets, ensuring a child's future, or leaving a legacy to a cherished cause.

1.4 WHY TRUSTS MATTER: THE CORE BENEFITS

Trusts stand as one of the most effective tools for asset protection, offering a robust shield against creditors and legal challenges. Within a trust, protections like spendthrift provisions play a crucial role. These provisions prevent beneficiaries from recklessly spending their inheritance or having it seized by creditors. Essentially, they ensure that the wealth remains secure and is used as intended by the grantor.

In the turbulent waters of divorce, trusts provide a safe harbor. Assets held in a trust can also be shielded from marital property claims, safeguarding family wealth from potential division. This protection is vital for anyone concerned about the impact of a divorce on their financial legacy. When you place your assets in a trust, this sets up a way you can preserve and convey your wealth to future generations, free from the reach of external threats.

The tax efficiency offered by trusts is another compelling reason to consider them. Trusts can help minimize estate taxes, allowing more of your wealth to reach your beneficiaries. By strategically placing assets in a trust, you can reduce the taxable portion of your estate, potentially saving significant amounts in taxes. Trusts also provide income tax benefits for beneficiaries. Specific types of trusts can distribute income in a way that takes advantage of lower tax brackets, reducing the overall tax burden on the family.

This strategic distribution ensures that your beneficiaries receive the maximum benefit from the assets you've worked hard to accumulate. Through careful planning, trusts make it possible to preserve wealth in a tax-efficient manner.

Control over asset distribution is a hallmark of the best trusts.

Your best trust will provide a level of personalization that other estate planning tools simply cannot match. With a trust, you can tailor distribution plans to fit your specific wishes and the needs of your beneficiaries. When you build your best trust, you can elect staggered distribution of assets incrementally over a set time period. This lets beneficiaries receive support when they need it most. This will prevent impulsive spending and provide financial security over the long-term. Another option comes with conditional distributions that get triggered by specific life events like a birthdate or perhaps even an educational milestone.

Trusts provide significant emotional and psychological relief. Knowing that your financial legacy is secure and that your wishes will be honored offers peace of mind that is invaluable. Your trust will enable you to protect vulnerable family members, ensuring they are cared for even when you are no longer around.

This assurance can alleviate worry and stress, allowing you to focus on enjoying life with the confidence that your loved ones are provided for. For those with complex family situations, building the right trust will serve as a stabilizing force, reducing the potential for disputes and fostering harmony among heirs. By establishing a trust, you create a plan that offers security and stability, both financially and emotionally, for generations to come.

This concludes Chapter One.

In summary, trusts offer a comprehensive suite of benefits that extend beyond mere financial considerations. They provide robust asset protection, tax efficiency, and unparalleled control over asset distribution.

More importantly, they deliver peace of mind and the assurance that your legacy will endure. As you consider the role of trusts in your estate planning, reflect on the profound impact they can have on your financial security and family well-being. Trusts are not just legal instruments; they are a clear declaration of your love and care for your heirs.

In the next chapter, we will take a look at different types of trusts and talk about the things you must consider when choosing the right trust type for your needs.

Meeting with qualified professionals will help you get started

CHAPTER 2
CHOOSING THE RIGHT TRUST

Imagine a situation where a family, after years of hard work, finally accumulates a significant amount of wealth. They plan to use it to secure their children's education and future. However, a lawsuit emerges seemingly out of nowhere, threatening to claim everything they've built. This is where understanding the distinction between revocable and irrevocable trusts becomes crucial. While both serve as protective financial instruments, knowing which one to choose can mean the difference between safeguarding your family's future or facing unexpected financial exposure.

2.1 REVOCABLE OR IRREVOCABLE TRUSTS?

Revocable and irrevocable trusts are opposite and exclusive. One is designed to be permanent and unchangeable unless dissolved altogether. The other allows the grantor to change it when he pleases. A revocable trust, often called a living trust, offers flexibility. It allows the grantor to modify or even dissolve the trust at any point during his lifetime. This flexibility makes it an attractive option for those who foresee changes in their assets or family circumstances. However, this convenience comes at a cost. Revocable trusts provide no protections against creditors. Also, as the grantor, you will be subject to taxation because a revocable trust retains all assets as part of the grantor's taxable estate.

In contrast, irrevocable trusts lock in the terms, once established, offering robust asset protection and potential estate tax advantages. The only way to dissolve an irrevocable trust is if all parties agree and sign a formal consent to dissolve. In some jurisdictions, a court order may also be required. This could involve a lengthy process with careful documentation. In short - irrevocable is hard to break.

Assets in an irrevocable trust are no longer a part of the grantor's estate. This insulates such assets from creditors and reduces estate taxes.

The suitability of one trust type over another depends largely on individual circumstances and goals.

Revocable trusts are ideal for those who wish to manage their assets while retaining control. This suits individuals who need to adjust their estate plans over time due to personal or financial changes, such as elderly persons who need to oversee their finances without relinquishing control entirely.

Irrevocable trusts, on the other hand, are better suited for individuals seeking long-term asset protection and tax efficiency. Professionals at risk of lawsuits, such as doctors or lawyers, might find an irrevocable trust particularly advantageous. By placing their assets in such a trust, they can protect their wealth from legal claims while also leveraging potential tax benefits.

You can see how the decision to create an irrevocable or a revocable trust will have long-term implications for both the grantor as well as the beneficiaries.

Revocable trusts allow the estate's assets to remain accessible and manageable during the grantor's lifetime, which can be crucial for adjusting to life's unpredictable changes. However, because these assets are still considered part of the grantor's estate, they are also subject to estate taxes upon the grantor's death. This may not be ideal for those looking to minimize estate taxes.

Irrevocable trusts remove assets from the taxable estate, potentially reducing estate taxes. Additionally, irrevocable trusts can affect Medicaid eligibility positively by excluding the trust assets from being counted as part of the grantor's resources, thus aiding in qualifying for benefits.

Consider the case of a family facing potential creditor issues. They opted for an irrevocable trust to secure their assets. This decision effectively shielded their wealth from claims, ensuring that their children would inherit without the burden of unforeseen debts. In another scenario, an elderly couple chose a revocable trust to manage their finances as they aged. This choice allowed them to adapt to changing healthcare needs and provide for their grandchildren, all while maintaining control over their assets. These examples highlight how strategic trust selection can address specific financial challenges and goals.

Reflect and Plan: Choosing Your Trust Type

Take a moment to consider your current financial situation and future goals. Reflect on the following questions to guide your decision-making process:

- How much control do you want over your assets during your lifetime?
- Are you concerned about protecting your wealth from potential lawsuits or creditors?
- What are your primary estate planning goals? Minimizing taxes, ensuring asset protection, or maintaining flexibility?
- How might your family circumstances change in the coming years, and how should your estate plan accommodate these changes?

Use these reflections to help determine whether a

revocable or irrevocable trust best aligns with your needs and objectives.

2.2 LIVING TRUSTS: WHEN AND WHY TO USE THEM

A living trust stands as a versatile instrument that serves to streamline and simplify the intricate processes of estate management and asset distribution. At its core, a living trust is designed to manage and protect your assets while you are living but, at the same time, providing a quiet transfer of your assets to your beneficiaries after you are gone, all without the need for probate.

Probate is a court-supervised process for authenticating your will and distribute your assets. While probate usually adheres to the directions in the will, it can be both time-consuming and costly, with public proceedings that expose private family matters to public scrutiny. A living trust sidesteps probate and keeps your affairs private – protecting the confidentiality that many families value. This privacy not only shields your financial details from public records but also facilitates a smoother transition of assets to your heirs.

A living trust also maintains continuity in asset management. Should you become incapacitated, your designated trustee will manage your assets according to your instructions, ensuring that your financial affairs are handled seamlessly.

This is especially important to those who wish to ensure that their healthcare and personal needs are managed without court intervention. Moreover, a living trust provides the advantage of immediately transferring assets to your beneficiaries upon your death, avoiding delays that a probate process might introduce. Beneficiaries who rely on these assets for financial stability or ongoing expenses will be grateful to you for your living trust.

Unlike other estate planning tools, a living trust allows you to alter its terms as your circumstances change, whether it involves adding new beneficiaries, adjusting asset allocations, or even changing the Trustee. This could be very important to families with minors who might need a change in guardianship or to individuals with substantial real estate holdings that require active management. Real estate, often a major component of an estate, can be smoothly managed through a living trust, ensuring that properties are maintained or sold according to your wishes without the need for court intervention. This feature is particularly attractive for those who own multiple properties or rental units. A living trust makes it easy to manage properties and transfer them to heirs efficiently.

Consider the case of a family with minor children. Establishing a living trust allows them to designate guardians and set terms for asset distribution that align with their children's needs and future. For example, they might stipulate that funds are allocated for educational expenses or released at certain milestones in the children's lives, such as graduation or marriage. This level of control provides financial security and stability for the children in accordance with the desires of their parents. Another practical scenario involves individuals with significant healthcare considerations. A living trust can be structured to include directives for medical decisions, allowing the trustee to act on your behalf, ensuring that your healthcare preferences are respected and funded.

For those with expansive estates, managing asset distribution can be daunting. A living trust simplifies this by clearly outlining how assets should be allocated, reducing the potential for family disputes. Suppose an individual has an estate comprising various investments, properties, and personal belongings. By incorporating these into a living trust, they can specify exactly how and when each asset is to be distributed, whether it involves immediate transfers or staggered distributions over time. This clarity helps prevent misunderstandings among heirs, fostering harmony and ensuring that your legacy is preserved as intended.

A living trust is not just a legal tool; it is a comprehensive plan that addresses the complexities of modern estate management. By offering privacy, flexibility, and control, living trusts offer a solution for a wide range of needs and circumstances, including the protection of minor children or managing substantial assets.

2.3 TESTAMENTARY TRUSTS: PLANNING FOR AFTER LIFE

Testamentary trusts are unique tools in estate planning because they are established through a will and only come into existence upon the grantor's death.

Unlike other types of trusts that you might set up during your lifetime, a testamentary trust is essentially a provision within your will. This means that it is activated only after you pass away, providing a mechanism to manage and distribute your assets posthumously. The trust outlines specific instructions on how you wish your assets to be handled, offering control over their distribution long after you are gone. A testamentary trust in the provisions of your will lets you maintain oversight and dictate terms, ensuring your assets serve their intended purpose.

A testamentary trust lets you control how and when your beneficiaries access their inheritance. This may be especially important to young children or beneficiaries you feel may not be ready to manage a substantial inheritance. As previously mentioned, a testamentary trust may specify conditions on the distribution of assets. However, there is just one catch. A testamentary trust must go through probate because it is a subordinate part of your will. As previously stated, probate is lengthy and public; potentially delaying the distribution of assets and exposing your financial matters to public scrutiny. Otherwise, a testamentary trust will strengthen the provisions of your will if that is what you want.

Ideal candidates for testamentary trusts often include parents with young children who want to ensure their offspring are provided for in a manner consistent with their values and intentions. This type of trust can be tailored to provide for children's education and living expenses, gradually distributing assets as the children mature. It can also protect these assets from mismanagement, thus making sure your children will have the resources they need when they need them.

Individuals with specific distribution wishes, such as those who want to support charitable causes or provide for relatives without granting them direct access to the assets, may also find testamentary trusts beneficial. They stipulate how funds will be allocated, reducing the risk of anyone contesting your will during the probate process.

Consider the scenario of a couple with two young children. They have worked hard to save for their children's future, but they worry about what might happen if they were no longer around to guide them. By establishing a testamentary trust, they can ensure their children's education and living expenses are covered. They might set terms that release a portion of the funds each year or upon reaching specific achievements, such as college enrollment. A testamentary trust not only secures their children's financial future but also instills in them a sense of responsibility and planning.

Another example involves an individual wanting to support a cause close to their heart. Through a testamentary trust, they can allocate a portion of their estate to a charity, ensuring their philanthropic goals are achieved without impacting their family's inheritance.

In summary, a testamentary trust provides a structured framework for managing your estate after your death, offering both control and flexibility. They serve as a testament to your foresight, ensuring that your assets are used wisely and according to your wishes. While they require probate and may involve some public exposure, the benefits of guided asset distribution and protection from mismanagement often outweigh these drawbacks.

You should take a hard look at your personal estate planning needs as well as the needs of your beneficiaries. Then decide whether you need a testamentary trust.

2.4 SPECIAL NEEDS TRUSTS: SECURITY FOR DEPENDENTS

Special needs trusts are meticulously designed to cater to individuals with disabilities, ensuring they receive the support they need without jeopardizing their access to essential public benefits. These trusts serve a dual purpose: they preserve eligibility for government assistance programs like Supplemental Security Income (SSI) and Medicaid, while also meeting the unique needs of the beneficiary. A special needs trust is important to families with loved ones who might be vulnerable. It helps preserve their quality of life and their eligibility for public assistance systems. By carefully managing the funds within the trust, families can ensure their dependents are adequately cared for throughout their lives.

Maintaining eligibility for benefits like SSI and Medicaid is crucial for many individuals with disabilities. A special needs trust is structured to ensure that the assets held within it do not count against the income and resource limits set by these programs. This is achieved through strategic fund distributions that supplement, rather than replace, the benefits provided by public assistance. The trust can cover expenses not typically addressed by government programs, such as specialized medical equipment, personal care items, and recreational activities, enhancing the beneficiary's overall quality of life. This careful management allows families to provide additional resources without risking the vital support these programs offer.

The trustee over a special needs trust will sometimes face very complex issues. Trustees must navigate the delicate balance of managing the trust's assets while ensuring compliance with legal and financial regulations. This includes making decisions on disbursements that align with the beneficiary's needs and the trust's guidelines. Trustees of a special needs trust must also keep meticulous records, documenting all transactions and ensuring that distributions do not affect the beneficiary's eligibility for public benefits. This responsibility requires a deep understanding of both the beneficiary's personal needs and the legal framework governing special needs trusts. The success of your trust to safeguard the interests and well-being of your beneficiaries will hang on who you choose to be your Trustee.

Real-world applications of special needs trusts highlight their profound impact on the lives of beneficiaries and their families. Consider the story of a family with a child who has lifelong care needs. By establishing a special needs trust, they were able to provide for their child's specialized medical care, therapies, and educational opportunities without affecting their eligibility for critical government programs. This trust not only secured the child's current needs but also laid a foundation for their future well-being, ensuring that they receive continuous support as they grow older.

Another example involves a young adult with disabilities who, through a special needs trust, gained access to resources that enhanced his quality of life. The trust funded activities and services that promoted independence and personal growth, offering the individual opportunities he would have never had otherwise.

As you explore the intricacies of special needs trusts, you can easily see how this legal instrument plays a pivotal role in safeguarding the financial futures of individuals with disabilities. They offer a pathway to security and independence, allowing beneficiaries to thrive while maintaining access to necessary public assistance. By understanding the unique benefits and responsibilities associated with special needs trusts, families can make informed decisions.

This concludes Chapter Two. To summarize: We compared revocable and irrevocable trusts and the need to weigh keeping assets accessible and manageable during the grantor's lifetime against the need to avoid estate taxes. We described how a living trust can provide for your care in case you are incapacitated and clearly direct distributions of assets when you pass and compared this to a Testamentary trust that can be established through a will to only come into existence upon the grantor's death.

We also discussed special needs trusts designed for individuals with disabilities to preserve eligibility for government assistance programs like Supplemental Security Income (SSI) and Medicaid, while also meeting the unique needs of the beneficiary.

In the next chapter, you will become acquainted with the legal foundations and historical development of Trust Law and the fiduciary duties of a Trustee.

CHAPTER 3
LEGAL FRAMEWORK AND TRUST LAW

Put yourself in the position of a successful entrepreneur who decides to secure the future by establishing a trust. After spending countless hours researching the best most appropriate options, you get mired down in a quagmire of legal jargon and conflicting laws across different states. You are not alone. Many people find themselves entangled in the complexities of trust law, unsure how to proceed, overwhelmed by the learning curve needed to understand the legal framework. You don't have to be a lawyer; you just need to ask the right questions – and let your attorney find the answers. This chapter should help you start to unravel the intricate legal underpinnings that govern trusts.

3.1 THE UNIFORM TRUST CODE (UTC)

Trusts are grounded in both statutory and common law. The Uniform Trust Code (UTC) serves as a foundational model law in the United States, designed to harmonize trust law across various jurisdictions. Established by the Uniform Law Commission, the UTC incorporates provisions from existing legal resources like the Restatement of Trusts and the Restatement of Property, and it has been enacted in 36 states as of October 2022. The UTC outlines the creation, modification, and termination of trusts, as well as the duties and powers of trustees. The UTC provides a consistent legal framework for managing trusts across state lines. Understanding the UTC's principles can help you appreciate how trusts are structured, ensuring compliance and protecting your assets effectively.

The historical development of trust law has seen significant contributions from common law principles. These principles have evolved over centuries, shaping the way trusts are used today. Historically, trusts were designed to manage and protect assets, allowing individuals to pass on their wealth while maintaining control over its distribution. Over time, the legal nuances of trusts have been refined, resulting in a sophisticated system that balances the interests of grantors, trustees, and beneficiaries. This evolution underscores the importance of understanding key legal terms and concepts, such as settlor and beneficiary rights. The settlor, sometimes referred to as the grantor, is the individual who creates the trust, transferring ownership of their assets to the trustee. The beneficiary is the person or entity for whom the trust is intended, receiving the benefits of the assets as outlined in the trust deed. This document is a critical component of any trust, detailing the terms and conditions under which the trust operates.

Jurisdictional variations in trust law can significantly impact how trusts are administered. Each state has its own specific laws governing trusts, which can affect everything from the creation and management to the modification and termination of a trust. For example, some states have adopted the UTC, while others rely on their own statutes and common law precedents. This diversity means that understanding local laws is crucial, especially if you have assets or beneficiaries in multiple states. These variations can also have implications for interstate asset management, requiring careful consideration and potentially the involvement of legal professionals who specialize in multi-jurisdictional trusts.

Courts play a pivotal role in trust administration, particularly when disputes or modifications arise. Probate courts often become involved in trust matters, especially if there's a disagreement among beneficiaries or if the terms of the trust need to be adjusted. While the primary aim of a trust is to avoid probate, courts may still intervene if there are concerns about fair and lawful administration. Judicial modifications of trusts can occur when circumstances change, such as a beneficiary's needs evolving or the value of the trust's assets fluctuating. In these cases, courts assess whether the modifications align with the settlor's original intentions and the best interests of the beneficiaries.

Courts generally exhibit a high degree of deference to trust entities, reflecting their confidence in the legal foundation and framework that trusts represent. This respect is rooted in the high probability of compliance with the UTC and other established legal guidelines. Trusts are seen as robust legal instruments that, when properly structured, offer a reliable means of managing and distributing assets. The confidence that courts place in trusts underscores their importance as a cornerstone of estate planning, offering a level of stability and predictability that is essential for securing your financial legacy.

Reflection Section: Assessing Your Trust's Legal Foundation

Take a moment to reflect on the legal aspects of your trust. Consider the following questions to ensure your trust is aligned with the relevant legal framework:

- Have you reviewed the trust laws specific to your state and any states where your assets or beneficiaries reside?

- Does your trust comply with the principles outlined in the Uniform Trust Code or applicable local statutes?
- Are you familiar with the rights and responsibilities of the settlor, trustee, and beneficiaries as outlined in your trust deed?
- Have you considered how jurisdictional variations might impact the administration of your trust?

By addressing these questions, you can ensure that your trust is well-grounded in a solid legal foundation, providing peace of mind and security for you and your beneficiaries.

3.2 FIDUCIARY DUTIES: WHAT TRUSTEES MUST KNOW

At the heart of trust management lies the concept of fiduciary duty, a legal and ethical obligation that forms the backbone of a trustee's responsibilities. Trustees are required by law act in the best interests of the beneficiaries. The duty of loyalty requires trustees to remain impartial and avoid conflicts of interest, ensuring that no personal gain influences their decisions. This means making choices that reflect the best interests of the beneficiaries, without favoritism or bias. Alongside this, the duty of care and prudence compels trustees to manage the trust's assets with a level of diligence and caution akin to managing their own affairs. This encompasses everything from making informed investment decisions to maintaining the trust's financial health.

Trustees have a broad range of responsibilities that are crucial to the effective management of a trust. One of the primary duties involves investment management, where trustees must strategically invest the trust's assets to ensure growth and sustainability. This requires a deep understanding of market dynamics and an aptitude for making sound financial decisions that align with the trust's objectives. Accurate record-keeping is another vital responsibility, as trustees must meticulously document all transactions and decisions. This ensures transparency and accountability, and it provides a clear financial history that can be reviewed by beneficiaries or legal entities when necessary. Moreover, trustees are responsible for the timely distribution of assets according to the trust's terms, making sure that beneficiaries receive their entitlements as specified. This involves careful planning and execution to ensure that distributions are made without unnecessary delays or complications.

Failing to uphold these fiduciary duties can lead to serious consequences for trustees. Legal liabilities and penalties can arise if a trustee breaches their duty, whether through negligence, mismanagement, or self-dealing. Such breaches can result in lawsuits, financial losses, and damage to the trustee's reputation. The impact on beneficiaries can be equally severe, as mismanagement of trust assets can diminish their expected inheritance, disrupt financial plans, and create unnecessary stress and conflict. Trustees who fail in their duties may be required to compensate beneficiaries for any losses incurred, further underscoring the importance of fulfilling these obligations with care and integrity.

To effectively meet their fiduciary duties, trustees can employ several practical strategies. Regular audits and reviews of the trust's financial status and investment performance are essential, ensuring that the trust remains aligned with its goals and that any issues are promptly addressed. This proactive approach helps maintain the trust's integrity and prevents potential problems from escalating. Clear and open communication with beneficiaries is equally important, as it fosters trust and transparency. Trustees should provide regular updates on the trust's performance and any significant decisions that affect the beneficiaries. This not only keeps beneficiaries informed but also reinforces their confidence in the trustee's ability to manage the trust effectively.

A Trustee's Journey to Success

A trustee who manages a family trust with multiple beneficiaries succeeds by prioritizing open communication. He regularly updates the family on investment decisions and trust performance. His proactive approach includes quarterly audits, ensuring the trust remains on track to meet its financial goals. His transparency and diligence foster trust and harmony among the beneficiaries. Your Trustee can have a positive impact on the lives of all your family members simple by paying attention and completing his fiduciary duties.

The role of a trustee is both challenging and rewarding. By understanding and embracing their fiduciary duties, trustees can make a meaningful difference in the lives of the beneficiaries they serve. Through careful planning, ethical decision-making, and clear communication, trustees can navigate the complexities of trust management and uphold the trust's integrity.

3.3 NAVIGATING PROBATE AND ESTATE TAXES

Probate is the legal process that must take place when someone passes away. It involves validating the deceased person's will and overseeing the distribution of their assets. The purpose is to ensure that the deceased's debts are paid and that the remaining assets are distributed according to their will. However, probate comes with its challenges. It can be time-consuming and costly, often resulting in delays that can be frustrating for beneficiaries. The process requires court proceedings, which can include filing forms, reporting assets, and attending hearings. These steps not only extend the time it takes for beneficiaries to receive their inheritance but also add to the burden of legal fees and court costs.

Trusts offer a strategic advantage in avoiding the cumbersome probate process, allowing for more efficient asset distribution. A revocable living trust is particularly effective in this regard. Unlike a will, a living trust does not require probate, meaning that the assets can be transferred to beneficiaries more quickly and privately. This keeps the financial affairs of the deceased confidential, away from public records. Moreover, trusts can include transfer-on-death arrangements, which automatically transfer specified assets to designated beneficiaries upon the grantor's death. This bypasses the need for probate entirely, ensuring a seamless transition of assets. By setting up a trust, you can save your loved ones from the stress and delays associated with probate, allowing them to focus on healing and honoring your legacy.

Estate taxes pose another significant consideration in estate planning. These are taxes imposed on the transfer of the deceased's estate and can significantly reduce the amount that beneficiaries ultimately receive. However, with careful planning, trusts can be structured to minimize these tax liabilities. For instance, the federal estate tax exemption allows individuals to transfer a certain amount of their estate free from federal estate taxes. By utilizing this exemption strategically, you can shield a portion of your estate from taxation. Irrevocable trusts are another powerful tool in tax planning. Assets placed in an irrevocable trust are typically removed from the taxable estate, reducing the overall estate size and, consequently, the estate tax liability. This approach not only preserves more wealth for your beneficiaries but also aligns with your financial and legacy goals.

Consider the example of a family that set up a family trust to manage their assets. By transferring their wealth into the trust, they effectively reduced the size of their taxable estate, thereby minimizing their estate tax burden. This strategic move not only preserved more of their wealth for their heirs but also ensured that their legacy was protected. In another scenario, a philanthropically-minded individual established a charitable trust. By doing so, they were able to provide for their favorite causes while enjoying significant tax deductions during their lifetime. These cases illustrate how trusts can be utilized not only to avoid probate but also to manage and reduce estate taxes effectively.

In navigating probate and estate taxes, trusts emerge as invaluable tools. They provide a pathway to protect and distribute assets efficiently, safeguarding them against unnecessary legal processes and tax liabilities. By understanding and leveraging the benefits of trusts, you can ensure a smoother transition of your estate, keeping your financial legacy intact for future generations.

3.4 COMMON LEGAL MISSTEPS AND HOW TO AVOID THEM

Creating and managing a trust involves numerous details, each of which can significantly impact the effectiveness of your estate plan. One common mistake is leaving trust documents incomplete or allowing them to become outdated. Life changes—such as marriage, divorce, the birth of a child, or significant shifts in financial status—necessitate updates to your trust to ensure it aligns with your current intentions. Failing to address these changes can lead to unintended consequences, such as assets being distributed to the wrong individuals or in a manner that no longer reflects your wishes. Another frequent error is the misidentification of beneficiaries. This can occur when names are misspelled or when beneficiaries are not properly defined, leading to confusion and potential legal battles over the rightful distribution of assets.

To prevent these pitfalls, it's crucial to engage in regular legal reviews and updates of your trust documents. Set a schedule to revisit your estate plan annually or after any significant life event, ensuring that all information remains accurate and relevant. This proactive approach helps maintain clarity and prevents disputes among beneficiaries. Additionally, clear and precise drafting of trust terms is essential. Ambiguities in the language can open the door to misinterpretation, potentially leading to legal challenges. Work with your attorney to ensure that your trust's terms are explicit and leave no room for misunderstanding. This clarity not only protects your intentions but also provides peace of mind to your beneficiaries.

The role of professional guidance cannot be overstated in avoiding these common mistakes. Consulting with an estate planning attorney can provide invaluable insights into the complexities of trust law, ensuring that your documents meet all legal requirements and reflect your intentions accurately. Similarly, engaging with tax advisors can help navigate the intricacies of tax planning, preventing unforeseen financial burdens on your estate and beneficiaries. These experts provide a safety net of knowledge and experience, guiding you through the trust creation process and helping you avoid costly errors.

Consider the cautionary tale of a family who neglected to update their trust after the birth of a second child. The original trust only mentioned their firstborn, leaving the second child with no legal claim to the estate. This oversight led to a contested trust, legal battles, and familial discord. Another example involves a trust where the terms were vaguely defined, leading to disputes over whether certain assets should be distributed immediately or held in trust for future generations. These real-life scenarios serve as reminders that even well-intentioned plans can unravel without careful attention to detail and regular maintenance.

To summarize key points from this chapter:

1. A trust is governed by the Uniform Trust Code (UTC) which outlines the creation, modification, and termination of trusts, as well as the duties and powers of trustees.

2. A Trustee has a broad range of responsibilities that are crucial to the effective management of a trust.

3. A trust can help you avoid probate and reduce your tax burden.

4. You want to get qualified professionals to help you avoid legal missteps and costly tax penalties.

In the next chapter, we will explore how to find the right professionals.

"Building The Best Trust" – your roadmap through the fog and confusion

CHAPTER 4

FINDING THE RIGHT PROFESSIONAL HELP

Imagine you are stopped on a lonely road deciding which way to turn at a vaguely marked crossroad. You can't see the fog covered road in front of you, and your GPS just lost signal.

A friendly face pulls up beside you and rolls down his car window. You accept the invitation and roll down yours. He hands you a map book and says, "Read this. It will help you decide where you want to be. Until you know that, it doesn't matter which way you go." He smiles, rolls up his window and drives away.

This is your map book. It can point the way and help you get the help you need.

4.1 TRUST ATTORNEY – YOUR PROFESSIONAL PARTNER

Choosing the right professional guidance can transform uncertainty into clarity. Choosing a trust attorney is not just about finding someone who knows the law; it's about partnering with a professional who understands your unique needs and can guide you through the intricate world of estate planning. It's about protecting your legacy and securing your family's financial future.

Selecting a trust attorney begins with assessing their qualifications and experience. You'll want to look for someone with a strong specialization in estate planning and trust law. This specialization ensures that they are well-versed in the nuances of trust management and the legal frameworks that govern it. Years of experience practicing trust law are equally important, as they provide the attorney with a depth of knowledge and a wealth of practical insights.

Membership in professional legal organizations, such as the American Bar Association or state-specific bar associations, can also indicate a commitment to staying current with legal developments and best practices in the field. These affiliations often require ongoing education, ensuring the attorney remains informed about the latest changes and trends in estate planning.

Communication is another crucial factor when choosing a trust attorney. The ability to explain complex legal terms in layman's language is invaluable. You need someone who can translate legal jargon into understandable concepts, empowering you to make informed decisions about your estate plan. An attorney's responsiveness to client queries also speaks volumes about their dedication and client-centered approach.

Whether through phone calls, emails, or face-to-face meetings, timely and clear communication is essential for building trust and ensuring that your questions and concerns are addressed promptly.

You want to find the professional who will give you this quality level of engagement. This not only fosters a positive working relationship but also ensures that you remain informed and confident throughout the trust-building process. Not only that, it is a clear indication of the level of support you may expect throughout the life of your Trust.

Reputation and client feedback are powerful tools in evaluating potential attorneys. Online reviews and ratings can provide insight into an attorney's track record and client satisfaction. Look for patterns in the feedback—consistent praise for professionalism, expertise, and client service can be reassuring. Referrals from friends or family who have navigated similar estate planning journeys can also offer valuable perspectives. Personal recommendations often come with firsthand accounts of the attorney's strengths and any potential drawbacks, helping you make a more informed decision. Additionally, consider asking the attorney for references or case studies that demonstrate their experience and success in handling cases similar to yours.

Understanding fee structures and ensuring they align with your budget is another critical step in selecting a trust attorney. Attorneys may charge flat fees for specific services, hourly rates for ongoing work, or even a percentage of the estate's value in some cases. Each structure has its advantages and potential drawbacks. Flat fees can provide predictability, allowing you to budget for services without worrying about unexpected costs. Hourly rates offer flexibility, especially if your needs are likely to evolve over time. Retainer agreements can combine elements of both, providing ongoing access to legal services for a predetermined fee.

You need to ask these questions when you interview with potential attorneys. Don't be bashful. Politely ask for clarity about the fee structure. Understand what it covers. Ask pointed questions about additional costs that might arise. Transparency in fees not only helps you plan financially but also sets clear expectations for the professional relationship.

The following 'Reflection Section' is designed to prompt thoughtful engagement with potential attorneys, ensuring that you find a professional who aligns with your needs and goals.

Reflection Section:

Questions to Ask a Potential Trust Attorney

- What experience do you have with cases similar to mine?
- How do you approach long-term estate planning?
- What is your availability for ongoing support and consultation?
- Can you provide examples of how you've handled complex trust issues?

4.2 THE ROLE OF FINANCIAL ADVISORS IN TRUST MANAGEMENT

When you think about managing a trust, financial advisors might not be the first professionals that come to mind. However, they play a pivotal role in ensuring that the trust's assets are not only preserved but also grow over time. One of the primary contributions of a financial advisor is in asset allocation and investment strategy. They assess the trust's objectives and the beneficiaries' needs, crafting a tailored investment portfolio that balances risk and return. By diversifying investments across various asset classes, they help protect the trust's assets from market volatility while aiming for growth. This strategic allocation ensures that the trust can meet its long-term obligations to beneficiaries, whether it's providing income, funding education, or supporting other financial goals.

In addition to creating an investment strategy, financial advisors continuously monitor the financial performance of trust assets. This ongoing oversight is crucial, as it allows for adjustments in response to market changes or shifts in the beneficiaries' needs. Advisors analyze performance metrics, review the economic landscape, and tweak the portfolio as necessary to align with the trust's objectives. Regular performance reviews ensure that the trust remains on track to meet its goals, providing peace of mind to both trustees and beneficiaries. By keeping a close watch on the assets, advisors help to mitigate risks and maximize the potential for returns.

The importance of choosing a fiduciary financial advisor cannot be overstated. A fiduciary is legally obligated to act in your best interest, prioritizing your needs above their own financial gain. This duty of loyalty is critical in trust management, where the stakes are high, and the consequences of mismanagement can be significant. A fiduciary advisor is committed to transparency and ethical decision-making, ensuring that the trust's assets are managed with integrity. This dedication builds trust with clients, offering reassurance that the advisor's recommendations are made with the best interests of the trust and its beneficiaries in mind.

Financial advisors often work in tandem with attorneys to give their clients a comprehensive estate planning package. This collaboration is key to aligning financial strategies with legal requirements, creating a cohesive plan that addresses all aspects of trust management. Advisors and attorneys coordinate estate planning strategies, ensuring that the financial and legal components of the trust complement each other.

Joint meetings with clients provide an opportunity to discuss the interplay between investment strategies and legal structures, offering a comprehensive view of the trust's objectives. This partnership ensures that all elements of the trust are considered, from tax implications to asset protection, creating a robust plan that stands the test of time.

Selecting the right financial advisor for your trust involves careful consideration of several factors. Credentials such as Certified Financial Planner (CFP) or Chartered Financial Analyst (CFA) designations indicate a high level of expertise and commitment to professional standards. These qualifications ensure that the advisor has the knowledge and skills necessary to manage complex financial situations. Additionally, compatibility with your financial goals is crucial. You'll want to find an advisor who understands your vision for the trust and can tailor their approach to meet your specific needs. This alignment is essential for building a successful working relationship, ensuring that the advisor's strategies reflect your priorities and values.

Ultimately, the role of a financial advisor in trust management is multifaceted, encompassing investment strategy, performance monitoring, and collaboration with legal professionals. By choosing a qualified fiduciary advisor, you can ensure that your trust's assets are managed with care and expertise, providing security and stability for your beneficiaries.

4.3 DECODING THE LEGAL JARGON WITH PROFESSIONAL HELP

Navigating the labyrinth of legal jargon in trust documents can sometimes feel like deciphering an ancient language. Trust agreements often abound with complex terms that are second nature to attorneys but daunting for those unfamiliar with legalese. This complexity can create barriers to understanding, potentially leading to costly misunderstandings or errors in trust management. When terms like "fiduciary duty" or "irrevocable trust" appear, they might seem impenetrable without a guide. Misinterpretations of these terms can result in incorrect trust setup or misaligned expectations among beneficiaries, which is why comprehension is not just beneficial—it's necessary. Misunderstandings can ripple into legal disputes, impacting the trust's effectiveness and the harmony among those it aims to benefit.

Professionals, particularly attorneys and financial advisors, serve as translators in this context, taking the mystery out of convoluted language and making it accessible. They have the expertise to break down complex legal terms into plain language, offering clarity where confusion might otherwise reign.

For example, an attorney can explain that a "grantor" is simply the person who creates the trust, transferring assets into it, while a "beneficiary" is the individual entitled to benefit from those assets. By providing such translations, these professionals help you grasp the essentials without requiring a legal background.

Additionally, many advisors offer educational sessions tailored to clients' needs, where they walk through the trust documentation step by step, highlighting key terms and their implications. These sessions can be invaluable in empowering you with the knowledge needed to make informed decisions about your estate planning.

For those eager to enhance their understanding of legal jargon, several strategies can be incredibly effective. One straightforward approach is to request written explanations from your attorney or advisor. This not only provides a reference you can revisit but also ensures that you have a clear understanding of the terms and their context.

Moreover, utilizing legal glossaries and resources, often available online or through your advisor's office, can further aid in comprehension. These glossaries provide concise definitions and explanations of common legal terms, serving as handy tools for decoding complex language. Engaging with these resources can bolster your confidence in navigating trust documents, transforming what once felt like an overwhelming task into a manageable one.

Clear communication, fostered by a solid grasp of legal terminology, significantly enhances trust management. When you understand the language of your trust, you are better positioned to engage in informed decision-making. You can confidently discuss your estate planning goals with your attorney, ensuring that your trust aligns with your intentions and the needs of your beneficiaries.

This informed perspective allows you to anticipate potential challenges and address them proactively, reducing the likelihood of legal disputes. A clear transparency regarding the terms in your trust will also foster trust among beneficiaries. As they can see the trust is being managed according to agreed-upon guidelines –. this not only prevents misunderstandings but also builds confidence in the trust's administration.

In the world of trusts, knowledge truly is power. By taking the time to decode legal jargon with the help of professionals, you equip yourself with the tools necessary to manage your trust effectively. This understanding not only safeguards your assets but also ensures that your estate planning objectives are realized, providing security and peace of mind for you and your beneficiaries.

4.4 BUILDING YOUR ADVISORY TEAM: WHO YOU NEED

In the realm of trust management, building a strong advisory team is akin to assembling a crew for a long voyage. Each member brings unique skills and perspectives, forming a collective that navigates the complexities of estate planning. At the helm is the trust attorney, whose expertise in estate law guides the legal structure and compliance of your trust. This professional ensures that the trust is legally sound and aligns with your goals, guarding against potential pitfalls. Alongside the attorney stands the financial advisor, the strategist who manages the trust's assets. Their role involves not only crafting investment strategies but also ensuring the trust's financial health. They monitor market trends and adjust portfolios to meet the trust’s objectives, providing a steady hand on the financial tiller. Completing this triad is the tax specialist, who steers through the intricate waters of tax regulation. Their insights help minimize tax liabilities, enhancing the trust's efficiency and preserving more wealth for your beneficiaries. Together, these professionals form the backbone of an advisory team, each contributing to the trust’s success.

The efficacy of your advisory team hinges on seamless coordination and clear communication. Regular team meetings create a forum for discussing strategies, aligning goals, and addressing any challenges that may arise. This is where team members synchronize their thoughts and get on the same page together to foster a collaborative effort where everyone's insights and expertise are shared freely. Shared access to trust documents is equally important, providing each member with the necessary information to make informed decisions. This transparency allows for real-time updates and adjustments, ensuring that the trust remains agile and responsive to changing circumstances. Effective communication not only streamlines trust management but also builds confidence among the team, enhancing their ability to serve your interests and those of your beneficiaries.

Selecting the right professionals to join your advisory team requires thoughtful consideration. Start by checking references and past collaborations to gauge each candidate's reliability and compatibility with others. This step provides insight into their working style and ability to integrate into a team setting. Assessing interpersonal skills is also crucial, as the dynamics within the team can significantly impact its effectiveness. Look for individuals who demonstrate empathy, patience, and the ability to communicate complex information clearly. These traits foster a supportive and productive team environment, where members work cohesively toward common goals. By choosing professionals who complement each other’s strengths and can collaborate seamlessly, you lay the groundwork for a robust advisory team that can navigate the intricacies of trust management with confidence and competence.

The needs of a trust can evolve over time, necessitating ongoing evaluation and adjustments within the advisory team. Conducting regular performance reviews of team members helps ensure that they continue to meet your expectations and contribute effectively to the trust's objectives. These evaluations provide an opportunity to assess each member's contributions, identify areas for improvement, and celebrate successes.

Adapting team roles to changing trust needs is equally important, as it allows the team to respond to new challenges and opportunities. This might involve bringing in additional expertise or reallocating responsibilities to leverage individual strengths. By remaining vigilant and proactive in managing your advisory team, you can ensure that it remains aligned with your vision and capable of guiding the trust through any complexities that may arise.

Your advisory team is the cornerstone of successful trust management, providing the expertise and support needed to achieve your estate planning goals. By carefully selecting professionals who work together as a team, it will make it easier for you to build your best trust. It also frees up your time and energy to focus on the broader picture, knowing that your trust is in capable hands.

As you finish Chapter 4, remember that building a strong advisory team is not a one-time task but a dynamic process that evolves as your personal and family needs change. To summarize, the person you pick to be your Trust Attorney in effect becomes your professional partner. The financial advisors you choose will collaborate with your attorney to align financial strategies with legal requirements and build a cohesive plan for your best Trust.

How your trust is funded is very important. In the next chapter, we will look at various ways to fund your trust.

CHAPTER 5

FUNDING YOUR TRUST

Imagine a family whose members worked together for years, saving and investing. They talked about a trust, then started reading, studying, and researching reputable professionals. They finally agreed to move forward and set up a trust. They engaged well qualified advisors to review the family portfolio. It included real estate, stocks, and treasured family heirlooms. After a critical discussion, family members disagreed about which assets to include in the trust and how to allocate them strategically. For a time, it looked like this family might not be getting a trust, after all.

Funding your trust is essential. Without this, you have no trust. Carefully consider your assets. Consult your professional team for guidance on asset types, allocation strategies, and valuation methods. In this chapter, you will be introduced to the terms and strategies involved in funding a trust so you can be prepared to work with your professional trust advisors

5.1 UNIQUE ASSETS FOR UNIQUE PURPOSES

When it comes to funding a trust, a variety of assets can be included, each serving a unique purpose. Real estate properties are a common choice, offering stability and potential appreciation over time. By placing real estate in a trust, you can preserve its value and ensure it is passed on to your beneficiaries without the complications of probate. Bank accounts and cash reserves are also frequently included, providing liquidity to cover immediate needs and expenses. This ensures that your trust can meet its financial obligations promptly, without disrupting other assets. Investment portfolios, such as stocks and bonds, offer growth potential and can be tailored to align with the trust's long-term goals. By including these in your trust, you can leverage market opportunities to increase the estate's overall value. Finally, personal property and collectibles, such as art or jewelry, add a personal touch to your trust, allowing you to pass on cherished items to your heirs.

Strategic allocation of assets within a trust involves balancing liquid and illiquid assets to meet both short-term and long-term needs. Liquid assets, such as cash and easily marketable securities, provide immediate funds to cover expenses like taxes, legal fees, or emergency repairs on trust properties. Having a portion of your trust in liquid assets ensures flexibility and responsiveness to unforeseen circumstances. On the other hand, illiquid assets, such as real estate or private business interests, contribute to long-term growth and stability. These assets may require more time to convert into cash but often offer significant appreciation and income potential. By thoughtfully allocating assets, you can ensure your trust is equipped to handle both present demands and future opportunities.

Diversification is a cornerstone of sound trust management, helping to minimize risk and enhance returns. By balancing asset classes within the trust, you mitigate the impact of market fluctuations on the estate's value. For instance, if stocks in the trust experience a downturn, the stability of real estate holdings can provide a buffer, maintaining the trust's overall financial health. Adjusting for market conditions is another crucial aspect of diversification. Regularly reviewing and rebalancing the trust's portfolio allows you to capitalize on favorable market trends while reducing exposure to potential risks. This proactive approach ensures that your trust remains resilient and aligned with your long-term objectives.

Accurately assessing the value of assets being transferred into a trust is vital for effective management and planning. Professional appraisals for real estate provide an objective valuation, ensuring you have a clear understanding of the property's worth. This information is crucial for both tax purposes and equitable distribution among beneficiaries. Similarly, market valuations for securities offer insight into the current value of stocks and bonds, guiding investment decisions within the trust. By maintaining up-to-date valuations, you can make informed choices about asset allocation, risk management, and growth strategies. This diligence not only protects your estate's value but also ensures that your trust fulfills its intended purpose for generations to come.

Reflection Section: Evaluating Your Asset Allocation

Consider the following questions as you evaluate your trust's asset allocation:

- How much of your trust's assets are liquid, and how does this align with your short-term financial needs?
- Are your assets diversified across different classes to minimize risk?
- Have you conducted professional appraisals for all significant assets to ensure accurate valuation?

Reflecting on these questions can help you refine your asset allocation strategy, ensuring your trust is well-positioned to achieve its objectives.

5.2 PROPERTY AND REAL ESTATE IN TRUSTS

Transferring real estate into a trust involves a few key steps, each crucial to ensuring that the property is legally secured within the trust. First, you must execute a deed transfer. This process begins with preparing a new deed that names the trust as the property owner. You can choose between a quitclaim deed, which is easier and more common, or a warranty deed, which offers more protection but involves a thorough lien check and might incur higher costs. Once the deed is ready, it needs to be signed and notarized to affirm its validity. After that, the next step is recording the deed with the local government, typically at the county courthouse. This step officially updates the public records to reflect the trust's ownership of the property, ensuring that your intentions are clearly documented and legally recognized. Remember to notify your insurance provider of the change, as this can affect your property's coverage.

Transferring real estate to a trust also brings several legal and tax considerations. One potential impact is the reassessment of property taxes. Depending on local regulations, changing the property's ownership to a trust may trigger a reassessment, potentially altering the tax obligations. It's important to consult with a tax advisor to understand how these changes might affect your situation. Another consideration is capital gains tax. While a trust can help manage these taxes, particularly if the property appreciates significantly, the specifics can vary based on the trust's structure and the property's value at the time of transfer. Understanding these implications is crucial to avoid unexpected expenses and ensure that the trust's benefits outweigh any additional costs.

The benefits of holding real estate within a trust are substantial. One of the primary advantages is probate avoidance. By placing real property in a trust, you ensure that it bypasses the probate process, which can be time-consuming and costly. This not only accelerates the transfer of property to your beneficiaries but also keeps your estate's details private, away from public scrutiny.

Additionally, a trust provides streamlined asset distribution. It allows for direct and efficient management of the property, ensuring that your wishes are respected without the delays and complications that probate can introduce. This is particularly beneficial if you own multiple properties or if your heirs have specific needs or preferences regarding the property's use or disposition.

Consider a multi-generational family home that has been cherished for decades. By placing it in a trust, the family ensures that the property remains within the family, providing a stable home for future generations. This setup can include provisions for maintenance and usage, such as who is responsible for upkeep or how the property can be used.

Another example involves rental properties managed within a trust. This arrangement allows for consistent and professional management, ensuring that rental income is distributed according to the trust's terms. It can also facilitate the transfer of ownership and responsibilities if the original owner passes away or becomes incapacitated, ensuring continuity and minimizing disruption for tenants.

5.3 FINANCIAL ACCOUNTS AND INVESTMENTS: TRANSFERRING ASSETS

Transferring financial accounts into a trust is a crucial step in ensuring that these assets are managed according to your estate planning goals. The first step in this process is updating the titles of your bank and brokerage accounts to reflect trust ownership. This involves contacting your financial institutions and requesting the necessary forms to change the account holder's name to that of the trust. It's important to have the official trust documents and your identification on hand, as these will be required to verify the change.

Once the paperwork is submitted, the financial institution will update their records to indicate that the trust is now the account owner. This step not only secures the assets within the trust but also ensures that they are governed by the trust's terms, providing a seamless transition in asset management.

Notifying financial institutions of the trust arrangement informs them that the trust is now the legal owner of the accounts and that all future transactions should be conducted under the trust's name. This step is vital for maintaining clear records and ensuring that all account activities are aligned with the trust's objectives. By establishing this communication, you set the groundwork for effective management and oversight of the trust's financial assets. Financial institutions may have specific procedures for trust accounts, including additional security measures or reporting requirements, so it's essential to understand these protocols and comply with them to avoid any disruptions in account management.

Managing investment portfolios within a trust requires a strategic approach to align with the trust's goals. Begin by assessing the trust’s objectives and risk tolerance, which will guide investment strategy. It's important to diversify the trust’s portfolio, balancing growth-oriented investments with more stable assets to mitigate risk. Regularly monitoring the performance of these investments is crucial. This involves reviewing financial statements, evaluating market trends, and making adjustments as needed to ensure the portfolio remains on track to meet the trust's objectives. By staying informed about market conditions and being proactive in managing the portfolio, trustees can maximize the trust’s potential for growth while safeguarding its assets.

Tax considerations play a significant role in transferring and managing financial assets within a trust. Trust-held accounts have specific reporting requirements, including annual tax filings that detail income generated by the trust's assets. It's important to understand these obligations and ensure compliance to avoid penalties.

Additionally, adopting tax-efficient investment strategies can optimize the trust's financial performance. This might involve reallocating assets to take advantage of tax benefits or structuring distributions in a way that minimizes tax liability for the trust and its beneficiaries. By carefully considering the tax implications of your investment decisions, you can enhance the trust's overall financial health and preserve more wealth for your heirs.

The following are two examples of transferring financial accounts into a trust. One couple transferred their retirement accounts into a trust. They wanted to make sure these funds would be managed and distributed according to their wishes. In this way, they not only secured the future financial stability of their beneficiaries, but also benefited from potential tax advantages associated with trust-held retirement assets. Another person transferred his dividend-generating stocks into a trust, creating a reliable income stream for his heirs. These examples show how trusts can be used to manage and protect financial accounts.

5.4 ENSURING CONTINUOUS FUNDING: STRATEGIES AND TIPS

Once your trust is established, maintaining its financial health becomes a continuous endeavor. Regular cash infusions are a reliable method to ensure your trust remains well-funded. These infusions can stem from diverse income sources, such as rental properties or dividends from investments. By directing a portion of these earnings into the trust, you create a steady flow of resources that can be utilized for immediate obligations or reinvested to fuel future growth.

Additionally, reinvesting income generated by trust-held assets can significantly bolster the trust's financial position. Whether it's interest from bonds or profits from equities, reinvesting these earnings within the trust can help compound its assets over time, enhancing its value and stability.

Managing the financial sustainability of a trust can pose challenges, particularly when income streams fluctuate. Variability in income can lead to periods of shortfall, making it essential to plan for such eventualities. Establishing a reserve fund within the trust can provide a buffer, absorbing unexpected dips in income and ensuring that all financial commitments are met without disruption.

Another common obstacle is addressing unexpected expenses, which can strain the trust's resources. These might include unforeseen repairs to trust properties or unanticipated legal fees. Building flexibility into the trust's budget and maintaining a contingency fund can help navigate these challenges, enabling the trust to cover additional costs without compromising its long-term objectives.

Insurance products offer a strategic avenue for

supporting trust funding, providing both security and predictability. Life insurance policies, when assigned with the trust as the beneficiary, can infuse substantial funds into the trust upon the policyholder's passing. This arrangement ensures that the trust receives a financial boost precisely when it might be needed the most, safeguarding the trust's capacity to meet its obligations to beneficiaries.

Annuities, on the other hand, offer a steady income stream, which can be particularly useful for trusts that require regular disbursements. By incorporating annuities, you can ensure a consistent cash flow, mitigating the impact of fluctuating income and providing financial stability for ongoing trust operations.

Maintaining the long-term financial health of a trust involves a proactive approach and periodic vigilance. Regular reviews of the trust's financial status are crucial. These reviews allow you to assess the trust's performance, identify any emerging issues, and make informed decisions about future directions. Adjusting funding strategies in response to economic changes is also vital. Economic landscapes evolve, and aligning the trust's financial strategies with these changes can optimize its performance.

Whether it's reallocating investments in response to market trends or adjusting spending plans to reflect inflation, adaptability is key to sustaining a trust's vitality. This ongoing attention not only preserves the trust's assets but also ensures it continues to fulfill its intended purpose for the beneficiaries.

Remember our imaginary family we introduced at the beginning of this chapter? They were stuck in a disagreement about how to fund their trust? After careful study and listening to the advice of their Trust Advisors, they agreed on a working strategy the maintained diversity – and control over critical assets.

They also agreed on a method of continuous funding that would allow their trust to adapt and thrive with changes in real life circumstances. By incorporating diverse income sources, preparing for uncertainties, leveraging insurance products, and maintaining vigilant oversight, you can secure a trust's financial future.

To summarize, in this chapter, you explored the dynamic nature of trust funding. There are a variety of assets that can be transferred to your trust, each serving a unique purpose. Strategic allocation of assets within a trust involves balancing liquid and illiquid assets to meet both short-term and long-term needs.

Accurately assessing the value of assets being transferred into a trust is vital for effective management and planning. Professional appraisals for real estate provide an objective valuation, ensuring you have a clear understanding of the property's worth.

Transferring financial accounts into a trust is a crucial step in ensuring your assets are managed according to your estate planning goals. This requires updating the titles of your bank and brokerage accounts to reflect trust ownership. As you work with financial institutions to transfer your assets to your trust, you want to make yourself aware of specific procedures and additional security measures or reporting requirements and comply with them to avoid any disruptions in account management.

Finally, working with your financial advisors to evaluate options and strategies for continuous funding will keep your trust abreast with the times.

The next step in trust management involves understanding the responsibilities that come with overseeing a trust.

The next chapter discusses this in-depth.

Qualified Professionals will help you build and manage your trust.

CHAPTER 6
TRUST MANAGEMENT AND RESPONSIBILITIES

Consider what it would be like, stepping into the role of a Trustee, a position that carries the weight of both fiduciary responsibility and family trust. This stewardship requires a balance of financial acumen, ethical judgment, and effective communication. If you or someone you know has ever thought about what it takes to fill this role, then let following capture your attention.

A Trustee is more than just a title; it is a professional commitment that involves managing someone else's legacy with integrity and care. He or she is expected to manage assets wisely and distribute them according to the Grantor's wishes. The role of trustee is more than just managing assets; it demands faithful attention to the express wishes of the grantor balanced with safe guarding the interests and welfare of the beneficiaries. This chapter clarifies the duties of a trustee and examines the court's expectation of anyone who accepts this role.

6.1 DUTIES OF A TRUSTEE

At the heart of a trustee's role lies the responsibility to distribute assets according to the trust terms. This task requires meticulous attention to detail, ensuring that all distributions align precisely with the instructions laid out by the grantor. Whether the trust specifies regular income payments to beneficiaries or the release of funds upon certain life events, it is the trustee's duty to adhere to these terms without deviation.

This involves not only understanding the nuances of the trust document but also maintaining comprehensive records that track each distribution. Such diligence ensures transparency and accountability, reinforcing the trust placed in you by both the grantor and beneficiaries.

Communication with beneficiaries is another cornerstone of a trustee's responsibilities. Regular updates foster transparency and trust, allowing beneficiaries to understand how the trust is managed. This communication can take the form of formal reports, detailing financial performance and upcoming distributions, or more informal conversations to address concerns or clarify terms.

Effective communication helps manage expectations and can prevent misunderstandings or disputes. It is crucial to approach these interactions with empathy and clarity, ensuring that beneficiaries feel heard and valued. By maintaining open lines of communication, you help foster a cooperative relationship that benefits all parties involved.

Impartiality and fairness are essential principles for any trustee. You must act without bias, managing the trust with integrity and ensuring equitable treatment of all beneficiaries. This means making decisions based on the trust's terms and the best interests of the beneficiaries, rather than personal preferences or relationships.

Handling conflicts of interest is a critical aspect of this impartiality. If a situation arises where your interests might conflict with those of the trust, it is vital to address it transparently and seek advice if necessary. Upholding these principles not only protects the trust but also enhances your credibility and trustworthiness as a trustee.

Financial management is a key component of a trustee's duties, involving the oversight of investments and expenditures within the trust. This requires a keen eye for detail and a strategic approach to asset management. Reviewing investment performance regularly is essential, as it ensures that the trust's assets are optimally positioned to meet its goals. This might involve adjusting the investment portfolio in response to market changes or reinvesting income to maximize growth.

Additionally, approving and monitoring expenses is critical to maintaining the trust's financial health. This includes evaluating necessary expenditures and ensuring they align with the trust's objectives and provisions.

Ongoing education and awareness are crucial for trustees to stay informed about legal and financial developments affecting trust management. Attending workshops or seminars can provide valuable insights into new regulations, trends, and best practices.

Subscribing to industry publications keeps you abreast of changes in estate law and financial markets, equipping you with the knowledge to make informed decisions. This commitment to continuous learning not only enhances your skills as a trustee but also ensures that you are prepared to navigate any challenges that may arise.

By staying informed, you can confidently manage the trust, providing security and peace of mind to the beneficiaries. Answers to the following questions will help Trustees fulfill their responsibilities with diligence and integrity.

Reflection Section: Evaluating the Trustee's Role

Consider the following questions to assess your performance and identify areas for improvement:

- Are you consistently adhering to the trust's terms and communicating effectively with beneficiaries?
- How do you ensure impartiality and fairness in your decision-making?

- What strategies do you employ to manage the trust's financial affairs effectively?
- How do you keep informed about changes in legal and financial landscapes that might impact the trust?

6.2 MANAGING TRUST ASSETS: BEST PRACTICES

In managing a trust, the strategy for handling assets is as crucial as the assets themselves. A well-balanced approach to asset management maximizes value while minimizing risks. One of the most effective strategies involves diversifying the investment portfolio.

Diversification means spreading investments across various asset classes, such as stocks, bonds, real estate, and alternative investments like private equity. This approach reduces the impact of any single asset's poor performance on the overall trust. Spreading your positions across a variety of sectors and geographical regions will help you mitigate market volatility and economic downturns. It's about ensuring that the trust's financial health does not rely too heavily on one type of investment.

Periodic asset valuation is another key aspect of managing trust assets effectively. Regularly assessing the value of assets ensures that the trust's financial statements reflect current market conditions. This practice involves appraising real estate holdings, re-evaluating stock and bond portfolios, and staying informed about the fair market value of unique assets like art or collectibles.

Asset valuation provides a clear picture of the trust's net worth and helps in making informed decisions about asset allocation and diversification strategies. It also aids in identifying underperforming assets that may need to be replaced or reallocated to optimize returns. By maintaining an up-to-date understanding of asset values, trustees can better strategize for both current and future financial needs.

Regular reviews and adjustments are necessary to ensure that the trust's asset management strategies remain aligned with its goals. Quarterly financial reviews offer an opportunity to assess the performance of investments, evaluate the effectiveness of current strategies, and make necessary adjustments.

These reviews should involve a thorough analysis of market trends, economic indicators, and any changes in the beneficiaries' needs or circumstances.

Rebalancing the investment portfolio is often a part of this process, ensuring that the asset allocation remains consistent with the trust's risk tolerance and objectives. Rebalancing might involve selling off some assets that have performed well to reinvest in underweighted areas, maintaining the desired level of diversification.

Risk assessment and mitigation are integral to protecting the trust's assets. Trustees must continually evaluate potential risks and develop strategies to minimize their impact. Assessing market volatility involves keeping an eye on economic indicators and geopolitical events that could affect investment performance.

Implementing risk reduction strategies may include diversifying further into low-risk investments or purchasing insurance to protect significant assets. It's about anticipating changes and preparing the trust to weather financial storms. This proactive approach helps preserve the trust's value and ensures that it remains capable of fulfilling its obligations to the beneficiaries.

There are numerous examples of successful asset management in trusts that illustrate these principles. Consider a trust with a diversified portfolio that included equities, fixed income, and real estate. Over the years, the trustee regularly reviewed and adjusted the portfolio, responding to market shifts and economic changes. This diligence led to steady growth and stability, even during periods of market instability.

Another example involves a trust that strategically managed a real estate portfolio. Periodic valuations and proactive management preserved and increased the value of its real estate holdings. Trust assets continued to generate income – continuously funding the trust.

6.3 RECORD KEEPING AND REPORTING: STAYING ORGANIZED

Record-keeping is the backbone of trust management, serving as a vital component not just for maintaining transparency but also for ensuring legal compliance. The meticulous tracking of financial transactions is fundamental, as it provides a clear account of all inflows and outflows within the trust. These records serve as a safeguard, protecting both the trustee and the beneficiaries by documenting every financial decision made. This level of detail is necessary to maintain the integrity of the trust and to provide evidence of prudent management.

Moreover, maintaining open lines of communication with beneficiaries is equally crucial. This not only involves updating them on the financial health of the trust but also ensuring that their concerns and questions are addressed promptly. By keeping comprehensive records of these communications, trustees can offer reassurance and build trust with the beneficiaries, ensuring that everyone is informed and aligned with the trust's objectives.

Trustees are expected to maintain a variety of records, each serving a different purpose in the administration of the trust. Financial statements and transaction records are at the forefront, providing a detailed history of the trust's financial activities. These documents should include everything from bank statements and investment reports to receipts for any purchases or expenses incurred by the trust. Tax filings and documentation are also essential, as they ensure compliance with tax laws and regulations. Trustees must keep track of all tax-related documents, including returns, supporting schedules, and any correspondence with tax authorities.

These records not only facilitate accurate reporting but also serve as a defense in the event of an audit or dispute. By organizing and maintaining these documents, trustees can ensure that the trust operates smoothly and remains in good standing with regulatory bodies.

Reporting obligations extend beyond maintaining internal records; trustees must also fulfill certain duties to beneficiaries and authorities. Providing annual financial reports to beneficiaries is a key aspect of this responsibility. These reports should offer a comprehensive overview of the trust's financial status, including a summary of income, expenses, and distributions. This transparency helps beneficiaries understand how the trust is managed and reassures them of the trustee's diligence.

Compliance with tax reporting regulations is equally important. Trustees must ensure that all necessary tax returns are filed accurately and on time, reflecting the trust's financial activities. This requires meticulous attention to detail and a thorough understanding of the applicable tax laws. By meeting these reporting obligations, trustees uphold their fiduciary duty and maintain the trust's credibility and legality.

To effectively manage all the documents and records associated with a trust, trustees can leverage a variety of tools and techniques. Digital record-keeping software is an invaluable resource, offering a centralized platform to store and organize documents. These programs often include features like automated backups, search functions, and secure access controls, enhancing both the efficiency and security of record management.

Additionally, implementing a system for categorizing and storing documents can further streamline the process. This might involve creating folders for different types of records, such as financial statements, tax documents, and beneficiary communications, and labeling them for easy retrieval.

Checklist for Effective Record Keeping

- Maintain detailed financial statements and transaction records
- Keep copies of all tax filings and related correspondence
- Document all communications with beneficiaries
- Utilize digital record-keeping software for secure and efficient management
- Organize documents with a clear categorization system for easy retrieval

6.4 ADAPTING TO CHANGES: MODIFYING TRUSTS OVER TIME

In the dynamic landscape of life, trusts must sometimes evolve to remain effective and relevant. Changes in family dynamics are among the most common reasons to revisit and modify a trust. Perhaps a new child has been born, or a marriage has occurred, necessitating the inclusion of additional beneficiaries. Conversely, a divorce might require the exclusion of a former spouse from the trust.

These changes demand prompt attention to ensure the trust reflects the current realities and intentions of the grantor. Moreover, legislative changes impacting trust law can also necessitate modifications. New tax laws, alterations in estate regulations, or changes in legal definitions can all affect the terms and efficacy of a trust. Staying attuned to these legislative shifts is crucial, as they can have significant implications for the trust's operations and tax obligations.

When a trust requires modification, understanding the legal process is essential. One of the first steps is petitioning the court for modification, particularly if the trust is irrevocable, as these trusts cannot be changed without legal approval. This process involves submitting a request to the appropriate court, outlining the reasons for the modification and detailing how the changes align with the grantor's original intentions. Alongside this, obtaining beneficiary consent is often necessary.

Beneficiaries must agree to the proposed changes, ensuring that their interests are considered and protected. In some cases, this might involve negotiating terms to address any concerns or objections. By navigating this process carefully, trustees can implement necessary changes while maintaining the trust's integrity and purpose.

The trustee plays a pivotal role in facilitating modifications, acting as the intermediary between the grantor, beneficiaries, and legal system. This involves consulting with legal advisors to assess the implications of potential changes and ensure compliance with applicable laws.

Legal advisors provide valuable guidance on the feasibility of modifications and the best approach to achieve them. Once a plan is in place, the trustee must communicate these changes to the beneficiaries, explaining the rationale and expected outcomes. Clear and transparent communication helps manage expectations and fosters trust among all parties involved. By proactively managing this process, trustees can ensure that modifications are implemented smoothly and effectively.

Consider the scenario where a trust's terms need updating to accommodate new tax laws. For instance, recent changes in estate tax thresholds might prompt a modification to maximize tax efficiency. In such cases, trustees work closely with legal and financial advisors to adjust the trust's terms, ensuring compliance and optimizing tax benefits.

Another common modification involves adjusting beneficiary distributions due to life changes. If a beneficiary's financial situation changes significantly, the trustee might modify the trust to alter distribution amounts or frequency, ensuring that the trust continues to meet the beneficiaries' needs.

Adapting a trust to reflect changes in circumstances is a crucial aspect of effective trust management. It's about ensuring that the trust remains a living document, capable of evolving alongside the lives it impacts.

Trustees must remain vigilant and proactive, ready to address changes as they arise, and equipped with the knowledge and resources to implement modifications seamlessly. By doing so, they uphold the trust's purpose and ensure that it continues to serve the best interests of all involved.

In this chapter, we discussed the responsibilities of a trustee, emphasizing the importance of adaptability and proactive management. We looked at some best practices for managing assets in your trust.

Reporting obligations extend beyond maintaining internal records; trustees must also fulfill certain duties to beneficiaries and authorities. Providing annual financial reports to beneficiaries is a key aspect of this responsibility.

Compliance with tax reporting regulations is equally important. Trustees must ensure that all necessary tax returns are filed accurately and on time, reflecting the trust's financial activities.

Finally, it is important to remember to stay current with changing situations and make sure your trust continues to meet the needs of its beneficiaries.

In next chapter, we will talk about strategies for reducing estate taxes.

Congratulations!

You have reached the half-way point.

I am excited you decided to read this book.

I sincerely hope you have enjoyed your read!
Will you consider leaving a review?

Most people will choose books based on reviews.

With your help, this book can reach many people just like you who may be undecided, real people who just need to see your kind words of reassurance.

To Post a Review

Open this link and sign into your Amazon account:

https://Amazon.com/review/create-review?&asin=0999745255

OR

Scan this QR Code, and sign into your account.

- Benjamin Carter

PS. See you at the end of your read! If you want, you may include a selfie holding this book with your review.

CHAPTER 7
TAX STRATEGIES AND IMPLICATIONS

John is a diligent planner. He spent time and money to build a trust he was certain to secure his family's future. He had a friend who understood trusts to help him find a trust attorney and carefully allocate assets, appoint a trustee, and stipulate detailed distribution terms. Then, a year later he was blindsided by a staggering tax bill – because he and his friend misunderstood how trusts are taxed.

This imaginary scenario highlights the importance of talking with a Trust Tax professional who understands how trusts are taxed. You want to find someone who will not only make sure your trust protects your assets, but also avoids unnecessary tax burdens.

While a trust is designed to help reduce your taxes, it can backfire if you don't understand how it works.

7.1 MANAGING INCOME DISTRIBUTION AND TAX BURDENS

Trusts are taxed uniquely at both federal and state levels, distinct from personal income. Federally, the tax brackets for trusts compress quickly, reaching the highest rate of 37% at just over $15,000 of taxable income, which is significantly lower than individual thresholds. This means trusts can incur high taxes from a relatively modest income.

Additionally, a 3.8% net investment income tax may apply if the trust's income exceeds certain limits. State-level taxation varies, often based on factors such as the trustee's residency or where the trust was created. Some states impose their own income taxes on trusts, adding another layer of complexity. Understanding these nuances is essential in strategizing effectively.

The distinction between grantor and non-grantor trusts plays a pivotal role in tax responsibilities. In a grantor trust, the grantor retains certain powers, which results in the trust's income being reported on the grantor's personal tax return. This scenario often applies to revocable trusts, where the grantor maintains control over the assets but the tax burden falls on the grantor; any income generated by the trust is taxed at their personal rate.

Conversely, non-grantor trusts are treated as separate taxable entities. They pay taxes on retained income at the trust level. If income is distributed to beneficiaries, it is taxed on the beneficiaries' personal returns. This setup can lead to strategic tax planning opportunities, as the income may be taxed at lower rates depending on the beneficiary's tax bracket.

Navigating tax filing requirements is crucial for maintaining compliance and avoiding penalties. Trusts must file an IRS Form 1041 annually, reporting their income, deductions, and distributions. This form is akin to a corporate tax return, detailing the trust's fiscal activities.

For beneficiaries, Schedule K-1 is issued, outlining their share of the trust's income, deductions, and credits. This ensures that beneficiaries report the appropriate income on their personal tax returns. Filing deadlines typically align with individual tax deadlines, but extensions can be requested if needed. Staying vigilant about these requirements is vital to prevent costly oversights.

Consider a trust that retains its income versus one that distributes it to beneficiaries. Retained income is taxed at the trust level, often at higher rates due to the compressed brackets. Distributing income can shift the tax burden to beneficiaries, potentially reducing the overall tax liability if they are in lower tax brackets. For capital gains, trusts that realize gains on asset sales must also navigate their taxation. If the gains are retained, they are taxed within the trust; if distributed, they pass to beneficiaries.

Understanding this dynamic will help you plan for opportunities to optimize tax outcomes based on the trust's and beneficiaries' circumstances.

To enhance your understanding of these complexities, here's a reflective exercise. Consider the trust you plan to establish or currently manage. Reflect on these questions to guide your tax planning:

Reflection Section: Assessing Trust Tax Implications

- Have you identified whether your trust is a grantor or non-grantor trust, and do you understand the implications for tax reporting?
- Are you aware of both federal and state tax obligations for your trust, including potential additional state taxes based on trustee residency?
- How do you plan to manage income distribution strategies to optimize tax liabilities for your trust and beneficiaries?
- Have you consulted with a tax professional to ensure compliance and explore tax-saving strategies specific to your trust's situation?

By addressing these questions, you can navigate the complexities of trust taxation more effectively.

7.2 STRATEGIES FOR REDUCING ESTATE TAXES

Estate taxes, often referred to as the "death tax," can significantly impact the wealth you intend to pass on to your heirs. At the federal level, these taxes apply to estates exceeding a certain threshold, which Congress periodically adjusts. For 2023, this threshold was set at $12.92 million for individuals, meaning any estate value above this is subject to taxation. The tax rate can be substantial, potentially reaching 40%, which underscores the importance of strategic planning.

Additionally, gift taxes intertwine with estate taxes under the unified credit system, limiting how much you can give away during your lifetime without incurring taxes. Understanding the intersection of gift and estate taxes is crucial as it allows you to reduce the taxable portion of your estate effectively, thereby preserving more wealth for your beneficiaries.

One of the most effective strategies to minimize estate taxes involves the strategic use of trusts. A credit shelter trust, sometimes called a bypass trust, is a popular tool in estate planning. This trust allows you to take full advantage of the estate tax exemption by transferring an amount up to the exemption limit into the trust upon your death. The assets in this trust are not taxed when your spouse inherits them, preserving the exemption for future generations.

Meanwhile, a generation-skipping trust (GST) offers another layer of protection. It allows you to transfer assets to your grandchildren, bypassing the immediate next generation, thereby reducing the potential tax burden on your children and leveraging tax exemptions across multiple generations. These trusts are particularly advantageous in families with significant wealth, as they help manage and distribute assets over time without unnecessary tax erosion.

In addition to trusts, integrating gifting strategies into your estate plan can further reduce your estate's taxable size. By utilizing the annual gift tax exclusion, which allows you to give up to $17,000 per recipient per year without affecting your lifetime exemption, you can gradually transfer wealth to your beneficiaries without triggering gift taxes. Over time, these gifts can significantly diminish the overall value of your estate, decreasing the amount subject to estate taxes.

Furthermore, charitable giving through trusts can serve a dual purpose: supporting causes you care about while simultaneously reducing your taxable estate. Charitable remainder trusts, for instance, allow you to donate assets to charity while retaining an income stream during your lifetime, offering substantial tax deductions and potentially lowering estate tax liabilities upon death.

Consider the case of a high-net-worth individual who effectively used an irrevocable life insurance trust (ILIT) to minimize estate taxes. By placing a life insurance policy within this trust, the policy proceeds were excluded from the individual's estate, saving millions in taxes. This strategy not only reduced the estate's taxable value but also ensured that the heirs received the full benefit of the insurance payout, untouched by tax obligations.

Another example involves a family business employing a family limited partnership (FLP) to transfer business interests to heirs. This approach allowed the business owner to gift shares at a discounted value due to lack of marketability and minority interest, significantly reducing the taxable estate and protecting the family enterprise for future generations.

These examples illustrate how thoughtful planning and strategic use of trusts can dramatically reduce estate taxes, safeguarding more of your wealth for those you care about most. By leveraging credit shelter and generation-skipping trusts, incorporating gifting strategies, and considering charitable contributions, you can craft an estate plan that not only aligns with your financial goals but also respects your legacy.

7.3 TAX BENEFITS OF IRREVOCABLE TRUSTS

Irrevocable trusts present a compelling opportunity for those looking to mitigate tax burdens and protect their estate by removing assets from your taxable estate. Once assets are placed into an irrevocable trust, they are no longer considered part of your estate, effectively reducing the value subject to estate taxes. This shift can lead to significant tax savings, as the assets within the trust are insulated from the tax liabilities that would otherwise apply upon your death. By transferring these assets out of your estate, you not only safeguard them from estate taxes but also protect them from potential creditors, ensuring they are preserved for your beneficiaries.

Beyond estate tax advantages, irrevocable trusts offer a strategic avenue for income shifting. This involves transferring income-generating assets into the trust, where the income can be allocated to beneficiaries who may be in lower tax brackets. By doing so, the overall tax liability is reduced, allowing more income to remain within the family rather than being lost to taxes.

This approach is particularly beneficial for families with multiple beneficiaries, as it optimizes tax efficiencies across different income levels. This redistribution of income not only maximizes the financial impact of the trust but also aligns with broader family financial strategies, ensuring that wealth is preserved and grown effectively over time.

Irrevocable trusts are also instrumental in facilitating tax-efficient gifting strategies. They enable you to make annual exclusion gifts, where you can give a set amount—currently $17,000 per recipient per year—

without incurring gift taxes. This strategy allows you to gradually transfer wealth out of your estate, further reducing its taxable size.

Additionally, the use of Crummey powers within a trust allows beneficiaries to withdraw contributions for a limited period, qualifying the gifts for the annual exclusion. This mechanism supports the transfer of significant sums over time without triggering gift tax liabilities. By leveraging these gifting strategies, you can efficiently manage estate value, and make sure your wealth is conveyed to those you intend.

Maximizing estate tax exemptions is another compelling advantage of irrevocable trusts. Through the use of the unified credit system, you can strategically allocate your estate tax exemption to reduce potential tax burdens. By pairing this with irrevocable trusts, you ensure that your estate efficiently utilizes available exemptions, preserving more wealth for your heirs. This approach is especially valuable in high-net-worth scenarios where estate values exceed exemption limits. The strategic deployment of these exemptions within a trust can significantly influence the estate's overall tax profile, providing a structured and predictable means of managing tax liabilities.

Consider the application of dynasty trusts, which are designed to preserve wealth across generations by leveraging tax efficiencies inherent in irrevocable trusts.

These trusts allow assets to grow and be distributed to successive generations without incurring additional estate taxes, making them a powerful tool for long-term wealth preservation. Similarly, charitable remainder trusts illustrate another strategic use of irrevocable trusts.

These trusts provide a stream of income to you or your beneficiaries for a specified period, after which the remaining assets are donated to a charity. This arrangement not only supports philanthropic goals but also offers immediate tax deductions and reduces estate tax liabilities.

These examples underscore the versatility of irrevocable trusts in achieving both financial and personal objectives, highlighting their role as a cornerstone in sophisticated estate planning strategies.

7.4 COMPLIANCE AND REPORTING: AVOIDING COMMON PITFALLS

Navigating the landscape of trust management requires more than just understanding tax obligations—it's about staying diligent with compliance. Compliance with tax laws and regulations will protect the integrity and success of your trust. Non-compliance can lead to severe consequences, including steep financial penalties, increased scrutiny from tax authorities, and potential legal challenges.

Accurate records are critically important. It serves as a

foundation for compliance, ensuring that all financial activities related to the trust are documented and accessible for review. This meticulous approach not only helps in filing accurate tax returns but also protects you from accusations of misconduct or negligence. Every transaction, distribution, and financial decision should be recorded in detail, creating a clear trail that can be followed during audits or disputes.

Trusts have specific reporting requirements that need careful attention. Among these are estimated tax payments, which must be made quarterly if the trust anticipates owing more than a certain amount in taxes for the year. This proactive payment approach prevents underpayment penalties and ensures that the trust remains in good standing with tax authorities. Annual distributions reporting is critical. This involves detailing the income distributed to beneficiaries, which affects how much the trust owes in taxes and informs the beneficiaries of their tax obligations. Failure to report these accurately can lead to discrepancies in tax filings, triggering audits or penalties. By adhering to these requirements, you maintain the transparency and credibility of your trust.

Ensuring compliance involves adopting several strategic measures. Regular consultations with tax professionals are invaluable. These experts keep you informed about any changes in tax laws that might affect your trust and help you make decisions about your trust that comply with changing tax laws. They can help interpret complex tax codes and regulations, ensuring that your trust's activities align with legal standards.

In addition to professional advice, utilizing compliance software and tools can streamline the process. These technologies automate many aspects of record-keeping and reporting, reducing the risk of human error. By leveraging digital solutions, you can efficiently manage your trust's compliance obligations, freeing up time to focus on other critical aspects of trust management.

To highlight the impact of non-compliance, consider a trust that failed to file its annual tax return on time. The oversight resulted in significant penalties and interest charges, diminishing the trust's assets and straining its ability to meet beneficiary obligations. Another example involves a trust that inaccurately reported its distributions, leading to an audit. The scrutiny uncovered additional discrepancies, compounding the trust's tax liabilities and damaging its reputation. These cautionary tales underscore the importance of vigilance and accuracy in compliance efforts. They serve as reminders that diligence pays off, protecting both your financial interests and the trust's legacy.

This concludes Chapter Seven.

As we close this chapter on tax strategies and implications, it's clear that understanding and managing compliance is a key component of successful trust management. Compliance ensures not only adherence to legal standards but also the preservation of trust assets for future generations. With a firm grasp on compliance, you can confidently navigate the complexities of trust taxation.

As we turn to the next chapter, we will explore how trusts can be leveraged for asset protection and equitable wealth distribution, further enhancing their role in comprehensive estate planning.

Trusts offer a structured approach to safeguarding and managing business interests

CHAPTER 8
PROTECTING ASSETS WITH TRUSTS

Consider how you might feel if you were a successful surgeon, well-respected in your field, suddenly found yourself facing a malpractice lawsuit that threatens to dismantle the financial security you spent decades building. You diligently saved for your children's education and your retirement. Then you were completely surprised to discover your assets were vulnerable to creditors.

This example underscores the importance of asset protection trusts, which are designed to shield personal assets from creditors and legal claims. These trusts are not just for the wealthy; they offer peace of mind to anyone who wants to ensure their hard-earned wealth is protected from unforeseen liabilities. No matter where you see yourself, these asset protection strategies may help you.

8.1 ASSET PROTECTION TRUSTS: WHAT YOU NEED TO KNOW

Asset protection trusts (APTs) serve a specific purpose: to safeguard assets from creditors, legal actions, and other financial threats. By transferring assets into an APT, ownership is legally transferred to the trust, which is managed by a trustee. This separation of ownership provides a legal barrier between your assets and potential creditors, enhancing your control over the disposition of your assets.

There are two primary types of APTs: Domestic Asset Protection Trusts (DAPTs) and Foreign Asset Protection Trusts (FAPTs). DAPTs, available in 17 U.S. states, offer asset protection without requiring assets to be moved overseas. These trusts are structured as self-settled spendthrift trusts, where you can be both the settlor and a beneficiary to your own trust and protect your own assets while enjoying the benefits of the trust. FAPTs are set up in foreign jurisdictions (such as Belize, or the Cook Islands) which offer robust asset protection laws and greater privacy.

The legal framework governing asset protection trusts is complex but essential to their effectiveness. For DAPTs, each state has its own legislation dictating the terms and protections offered, with some states providing stronger creditor protections than others. For example, the Bankruptcy Abuse Prevention and Consumer Protection Act (BAPCPA) impacts how DAPTs are treated in bankruptcy proceedings. Statutory requirements for establishing an APT include irrevocability, meaning once assets are placed in the trust, they cannot be easily removed. This permanency is key to ensuring the trust's protections are reliable. In contrast, FAPTs rely on the legal systems of their respective jurisdictions, which often do not recognize foreign judgments. This means that even if a creditor obtains a judgment against you in the U.S., they may face significant legal hurdles in accessing the trust's assets overseas.

The benefits of asset protection trusts are numerous, particularly for individuals seeking to preserve their wealth against unexpected liabilities. One of the most significant advantages is the ability to shield assets from legal judgments, providing a layer of security that keeps your wealth intact in the face of lawsuits or creditor claims. This is especially valuable for professionals in high-risk fields, such as medicine or construction, where litigation is more common. Additionally, APTs help preserve family wealth by safeguarding assets intended for future generations, ensuring that your legacy remains protected. This security allows you to focus on your career and family, knowing that your financial foundation is fortified against potential threats.

Many people have used offshore trusts to protect their assets. By placing your wealth in a FAPT, you can maintain control over your assets while benefiting from stringent asset protection laws of a foreign jurisdiction. This not only safeguards your assets from domestic creditors but also provides enhanced privacy and estate planning advantages. Similarly, professionals at high risk for litigation, such as doctors, have successfully employed DAPTs to protect their personal assets. By establishing a DAPT in a state with favorable asset protection laws, they have been able to separate their personal wealth from potential legal claims arising from their professional practice. Maybe an APT is the right trust for you. Take a moment to reflect on your unique situation.

Reflection Section: Assessing Asset Protection Needs

- Evaluate Vulnerabilities: Consider the areas of your professional and personal life that might expose you to financial risk.

- State vs. Offshore: Determine whether a domestic or offshore trust better suits your asset protection needs, factoring in legal environments and potential threats.

- Long-Term Goals: Align your asset protection strategy with your long-term financial and legacy goals, ensuring that the trust structure supports these objectives.

8.2 LEGAL BARRIERS: KEEPING CREDITORS AT BAY

Asset protection trusts are powerful, but their effectiveness often hinges on specific legal strategies aimed at deterring creditors. One such strategy involves the use of spendthrift clauses. These clauses are designed to prevent beneficiaries from squandering their inheritance by restricting their access to the trust funds. Essentially, it shields the trust's assets from the beneficiary's creditors by limiting their ability to transfer or pledge future distributions. This ensures that the assets remain protected and are used as intended by the trust creator.

Another crucial legal tool is the discretionary distribution term, which grants trustees the authority to decide when and how much to distribute to beneficiaries. This discretion allows trustees to withhold distributions if they believe the funds could be at risk from creditors, thereby providing an additional layer of protection.

Understanding the concept of fraudulent conveyance is vital when establishing asset protection trusts. Fraudulent conveyance occurs when assets are transferred to a trust with the intent to hinder, delay, or defraud creditors. If a court determines that such intent existed, it can invalidate the transfer, leaving the assets vulnerable. To avoid this, it's crucial to ensure that asset transfers are executed well before any creditor claims arise and that the intent behind setting up the trust is legitimate and not solely for evading creditors. The timing of asset transfers plays a critical role; establishing a trust long before any financial distress or legal action can demonstrate good faith and legitimate planning. This foresight helps protect the trust from being challenged as a fraudulent conveyance, preserving its intended security.

Privacy is another significant component of asset protection. A well-structured trust can offer confidentiality that deters creditors from pursuing claims. Privacy provisions within trusts, such as confidentiality clauses, ensure that details about the trust's assets and beneficiaries are not disclosed without consent. This privacy not only protects sensitive financial information but also reduces the risk of creditors targeting the trust. Utilizing nominee trustees can further enhance anonymity. A nominee trustee holds the legal title to the assets on behalf of the actual trustee, adding a layer of separation that can make it difficult for creditors to trace and claim assets. This anonymity is particularly beneficial in jurisdictions where public records could expose financial holdings to potential threats.

To maximize the protection offered by trusts, consider taking proactive measures. The earlier you establish asset protection measures, the more robust your defense against creditors. Early planning demonstrates to courts that the trust was not created in response to immediate financial threats, reducing the risk of challenges.

Additionally, regular reviews of the trust structure and compliance with legal standards ensure that the trust remains effective and aligned with current laws. This involves consulting with legal professionals to assess and update the trust as needed, ensuring that it continues to offer maximum protection against creditors. Regular audits and updates help maintain the trust's integrity, adapting to any changes in your financial situation or legal landscape. By staying vigilant and informed, you can safeguard your assets and ensure that your trust provides the security and peace of mind you seek.

In navigating the complexities of asset protection, these legal strategies play a crucial role. From the strategic use of spendthrift clauses to maintaining privacy, each element contributes to a comprehensive defense against potential threats. By understanding and implementing these strategies, you can effectively keep creditors at bay and secure your assets for the future. Whether it's through careful planning, regular reviews, or strategic structuring, the right approach to asset protection can make all the difference in preserving your financial legacy.

8.3 TRUSTS FOR BUSINESS OWNERS AND ENTREPRENEURS

For business owners and entrepreneurs, the stakes are exceptionally high. The unique challenges they face demand tailored trust strategies that go beyond standard asset protection. Entrepreneurs often find themselves exposed to various risks stemming from their business operations. From potential lawsuits to fluctuating market conditions, these risks can threaten both personal and business assets. Additionally, succession planning is a critical concern. The continuity of a business hinges on a clear plan for leadership transition, ensuring that the business can thrive beyond the current owner's involvement. This is where trusts become invaluable, offering a structured approach to safeguarding and managing business interests.

Incorporating business assets into trust structures requires thoughtful consideration and precise execution. Business owners can place shares and ownership interests directly into a trust, effectively separating personal wealth from business liabilities. This separation ensures that personal assets remain protected, even if the business faces financial challenges. Trusts can also encapsulate comprehensive business succession plans. By embedding these plans within the trust's terms, owners can clearly outline how leadership and ownership should transition, minimizing disruptions. This not only preserves the business's operational integrity but also reassures stakeholders that the company is in capable hands, promoting stability and confidence among employees, clients, and investors.

Trusts provide distinct advantages by shielding business

assets from personal liabilities. By legally distinguishing between personal and business assets, trusts prevent creditors from accessing personal wealth to settle business debts. This protection is particularly crucial for entrepreneurs in high-risk industries, where the likelihood of legal challenges is significant. Furthermore, trusts ensure the seamless continuation of business operations. With a trust in place, day-to-day operations remain unaffected by personal legal issues, allowing the business to operate as usual. This continuity is vital for maintaining client relationships and market presence, as well as for ensuring that employees' livelihoods are not disrupted by unforeseen personal challenges faced by the business owner.

Consider the scenario of a successful family-owned corporation that employs a dynasty trust to preserve its legacy. By structuring the business within a dynasty trust, the family ensures that the company can be passed down through generations without the threat of estate taxes eroding its value. This approach not only protects the business's financial health but also honors the family's commitment to nurturing the enterprise over the long term. In another example, a sole proprietor might establish an irrevocable trust to shield their business from personal liabilities. This strategy allows the business owner to separate their personal finances from business risks, safeguarding their personal wealth while maintaining control over business operations. These cases illustrate how entrepreneurs can leverage trusts to secure their business interests, protect their personal assets, and plan for a future that extends beyond their direct involvement.

By understanding the unique needs and challenges faced by business owners, trusts can be tailored to provide targeted solutions. Whether it's through asset separation, succession planning, or liability protection, trusts offer a versatile and robust framework for managing business interests. The option for ensuring uninterrupted operations while securing both personal and business assets is why a trust can be an indispensable tool for entrepreneurs seeking to fortify their financial future.

8.4 SPENDTHRIFT TRUSTS: GUARDING AGAINST IRRESPONSIBLE SPENDING

Consider a young adult who inherits a sizeable sum from a family member. Without proper guidance, there's a risk of squandering it on impulsive purchases or ill-advised investments. This is where a spendthrift trust becomes invaluable. Designed to protect the assets from being frittered away, these trusts restrict the beneficiary's access to the funds. Instead of receiving a large, lump-sum inheritance, the beneficiary gets distributions at intervals or under certain conditions. This control lies in the hands of the trustee, who oversees how and when the funds are accessed. By doing so, the trust effectively safeguards the wealth, ensuring it's used wisely and in alignment with the grantor's intentions.

The legal enforceability of spendthrift provisions is robust, yet they do come with certain limitations. Courts generally uphold these provisions, recognizing their value in protecting assets from creditors and beneficiaries' poor financial decisions. However, state recognition varies, and some states may not enforce spendthrift clauses as strictly. Exceptions exist for specific creditors, such as those owed for alimony or child support, who might still access the trust's assets. These exceptions ensure that while the trust protects against frivolous spending, it doesn't shield beneficiaries from legitimate financial obligations. It balances protection with responsibility.

For grantors, a spendthrift trust offers peace of mind, knowing that their legacy is preserved over generations. It allows them to set specific terms for asset distribution that reflect their values, ensuring that wealth is not only protected but also promotes financial literacy and responsibility among beneficiaries. For beneficiaries who may struggle with managing money or have a history of impulsive spending, this trust provides a safety net. It offers financial security by ensuring they receive support without the risk of exhausting their inheritance. This structure helps those with challenges like substance abuse, where unrestricted access to funds might exacerbate their situation.

A practical scenario illustrates the power of spendthrift trusts. Imagine a family setting up such a trust for a young heir known for impulsive financial decisions. The trustee, perhaps a family member or a financial advisor, distributes funds incrementally, allowing the beneficiary to learn and adapt to managing their finances responsibly. This measured approach not only prevents financial ruin but also encourages the heir to develop healthier spending habits. Another case might involve a beneficiary with a history of substance abuse. Here, the trust ensures that funds are allocated for essential needs and potentially supportive interventions, protecting the beneficiary from the harm of unrestricted access to cash.

In essence, spendthrift trusts serve as a financial guardian, offering a structured approach to wealth management that secures assets against the risks of poor financial judgment. By managing how funds are accessed and used, these trusts provide a framework that fosters financial well-being and preserves family wealth. This chapter has explored the various ways trusts can protect and manage assets, ensuring they serve their intended purpose and benefit future generations. The next chapter talks about distribution strategies.

CHAPTER 9
EQUITABLE DISTRIBUTION STRATEGIES

Imagine sitting around a table with your family, discussing how to divide your life's work among those you love most. It's a conversation filled with hope, dreams, and sometimes, tension. The importance of equitable distribution in estate planning cannot be overstated.

A well-balanced distribution plan is not just about dividing assets; it's about preserving family harmony and respecting the values and intentions of the grantor. When assets are distributed unevenly or without clear reasoning, it can lead to conflicts among heirs, breeding resentment and fracturing relationships. Equitable distribution reflects the grantor's wishes in a way that honors their legacy and provides peace of mind for the future.

9.1 FAIR ASSET DISTRIBUTION

Several factors influence how assets are distributed among heirs, and understanding these is crucial for effective estate planning. The financial needs and stability of each heir should be a primary consideration. Some heirs may have greater financial responsibilities due to health issues, education needs, or their stage in life, requiring a more substantial share of the estate. Additionally, the contribution of an heir to a family business or estate often plays a significant role. An heir actively involved in maintaining or growing a family business might receive a larger portion to ensure continuity and reward their efforts.

Determining what is fair in asset distribution can be challenging, but several strategies can guide this process. Regularly assessing each heir's situation allows the grantor to adapt the plan as circumstances change. For example, if an heir achieves financial independence or encounters unexpected hardships, the distribution plan can be adjusted accordingly. Incorporating heir feedback is another effective strategy.

By engaging heirs in discussions about their needs and expectations, grantors can make informed decisions that minimize surprises and potential conflicts. These conversations can also help heirs understand the reasoning behind the distribution decisions, fostering a sense of inclusion and fairness.

Consider the example of a family with three adult children, each at different stages in their lives. The parents establish a trust that equalizes asset values through a combination of cash and property offsets. The eldest, who has taken over the family business, receives a larger share of the business assets, while the younger siblings receive equivalent value in liquid assets and real estate. This approach ensures that each child benefits according to their needs and contributions. In another scenario, a family prioritizes educational support for their younger heirs.

The trust provides specific funds for college tuition and related expenses, ensuring that the grandchildren have the resources they need to pursue their dreams. These examples illustrate how strategic planning can achieve equitable outcomes that align with the family's goals and values.

Reflection Section: Evaluating Your Distribution Plan

- Consider Each Heir's Needs: Regularly review the financial stability and responsibilities of each heir.

- Engage in Open Dialogue: Involve heirs in discussions about the distribution plan to understand their perspectives.

- Adapt to Changing Circumstances: Be prepared to adjust the plan as life events occur.

Thoughtful consideration will enable you to select a practical distribution strategy that strengthens family bonds.

9.2 DISCRETIONARY TRUSTS: PROVIDING FOR UNPREDICTABLE FUTURES

Discretionary trusts are a unique and powerful tool in estate planning, offering a level of flexibility that is particularly beneficial for managing uncertain futures. Unlike fixed trusts, where beneficiaries receive specific amounts or percentages at set times, discretionary trusts grant the trustee the authority to decide when and how much each beneficiary receives.

This discretion enables the trustee to respond to changing circumstances, ensuring that the trust's assets are distributed in the most effective manner. The trustee's role becomes one of thoughtful stewardship, balancing the immediate needs of beneficiaries with the long-term goals of the trust. This flexibility is crucial in scenarios where beneficiaries might face unpredictable life events, such as sudden illness, unemployment, or the need for further education.

The adaptability of discretionary trusts is one of their key benefits. Life is unpredictable, and the needs of beneficiaries can change rapidly. A discretionary trust leaves options open to respond to significant life events.

For instance, if a beneficiary marries or faces a health crisis, the trustee can allocate funds to support them during these times. This ensures that the trust remains relevant and supportive throughout the beneficiaries' lives. Additionally, discretionary trusts can provide for beneficiaries with special needs without affecting their eligibility for government benefits. This is accomplished by structuring distributions in a way that supplements rather than replaces public assistance, thereby enhancing the quality of life for those beneficiaries without compromising their financial support systems.

Trustees of discretionary trusts hold significant responsibilities and powers, requiring them to assess the needs and circumstances of beneficiaries regularly. This involves understanding the individual situations of each beneficiary, such as their financial status, health, and personal goals. Trustees must weigh these factors to make informed decisions about distributions, ensuring that they meet immediate needs while also preserving the trust's assets for future security.

This balancing act requires trustees to maintain a long-term perspective, considering the overall sustainability of the trust and its ability to fulfill its purpose over time. Effective trusteeship involves open communication with beneficiaries, ensuring they understand the reasons behind distribution decisions and the overall objectives of the trust.

Consider the case of a discretionary trust established for a beneficiary with unstable employment. The trustee, recognizing the beneficiary's fluctuating income, adjusts distributions to provide support during periods of unemployment, while reducing support when the beneficiary is financially stable. This approach not only provides a safety net but also encourages the beneficiary to seek stable employment opportunities.

In another example, a discretionary trust might be used to support a beneficiary pursuing higher education. The trustee can allocate funds to cover tuition and living expenses, adjusting the level of support based on the beneficiary's academic progress and financial needs.

Reflective Exercise: Assessing Trustee Discretion

- Evaluate Changing Needs: Regularly review the personal and financial circumstances of each beneficiary.

- Communicate Clearly: Ensure beneficiaries understand the trust's purpose and distribution rationale.

- Balance Immediate and Future Needs: Consider both short-term support and long-term sustainability of the trust.

Through these strategies, discretionary trusts provide a dynamic approach to managing assets, adapting to life's uncertainties while maintaining the integrity of the grantor's wishes.

9.3 FAMILY DYNAMICS

Navigating the complexities of family dynamics in estate planning can be akin to walking a tightrope, where each step requires careful consideration of diverse needs and relationships. Families often comprise individuals with varying interests and expectations, which can lead to unique challenges, especially when it comes to distributing assets.

Conflicting interests among siblings might arise when one feels more entitled due to their involvement in family businesses or differing life circumstances. Managing expectations across multiple generations further complicates matters, as older family members may prioritize preserving assets for the future, while younger heirs might focus on immediate needs. These nuances necessitate a thoughtful approach to estate planning, ensuring that all parties feel valued and understood.

One of the most effective strategies for addressing conflicts within families is the use of mediation and family meetings. These forums provide a safe space for open dialogue, allowing all parties to express their concerns and desires. Mediation offers an impartial perspective, guiding families toward mutually agreeable solutions.

Additionally, incorporating conflict resolution clauses in trust terms can preemptively address potential disputes.

These clauses could make stipulations such as resolving disagreements through arbitration rather than litigation, preserving family harmony and avoiding costly legal battles. By proactively addressing potential sources of conflict, families can establish a framework for peaceful and equitable distribution of assets.

Clear communication stands as a cornerstone in managing family dynamics effectively. Regular updates and reports to beneficiaries ensure transparency, keeping everyone informed about the trust's status and any changes that might affect them. This openness reduces misunderstandings and fosters trust among family members.

Establishing open lines of communication, where family members feel comfortable discussing their concerns and aspirations, further strengthens relationships. Encouraging beneficiaries to voice their thoughts can lead to more informed decisions and adjustments, aligning the trust's management with the evolving needs of the family. Transparency and dialogue not only prevent conflicts but also build a sense of unity and shared purpose.

Examples of successful conflict management in families often involve the thoughtful structuring of trusts and the appointment of neutral third-party trustees. Such trustees, free from familial biases, can oversee the trust's administration impartially, ensuring that the grantor's wishes are honored without favoritism. This neutrality can be particularly beneficial in families with deep-rooted tensions or complex dynamics.

Another approach is the implementation of structured family governance frameworks, where roles and responsibilities are clearly defined, and decision-making processes are formalized. These frameworks provide clarity and consistency, reducing the likelihood of disputes and ensuring that all family members have a voice in the estate planning process.

9.4 TRUSTS FOR BLENDED FAMILIES: ENSURING FAIRNESS

Blended families bring diverse needs to estate planning. They often involve balancing the interests of legacy children with those of new family members. This complexity arises from the need to address potential feelings of favoritism and ensure that each beneficiary receives their fair share.

When stepchildren and new partners are introduced into the family structure, traditional distribution methods may no longer suffice. Instead, a tailored approach to trust planning is necessary to accommodate the diverse needs and expectations of all involved. This might involve creating separate trusts for different branches of the family, ensuring that each group receives assets in a manner that respects their relationship with the grantor.

To achieve equitable trust design in blended families, several strategies can be employed. Proportional distributions based on family contributions can be an effective way to allocate assets fairly. For example, if one branch of the family has contributed significantly to maintaining a family business, they might receive a larger share of those assets.

Separate trusts can also be established for different family branches, allowing for customized distribution plans that reflect the unique dynamics of each group. This separation helps prevent conflicts and ensures that the grantor's intentions are clearly delineated. By tailoring trust structures to the specific needs of a blended family, the grantor can provide for all beneficiaries without compromising fairness.

Prenuptial and postnuptial agreements complement trust planning for blended families. Prenuptial agreements, established before marriage, and postnuptial agreements, created after marriage, outline how assets will be divided in the event of divorce or death. These agreements can clarify asset distribution prior to marriage, mitigating potential disputes among heirs.

Incorporating trust terms into these agreements can further reinforce the grantor's intentions, ensuring that assets are allocated according to their wishes. While these agreements provide clear guidelines, they also require careful consideration, as they may involve sensitive discussions about financial arrangements. However, when executed thoughtfully, they offer a robust framework for managing expectations and protecting the interests of all parties involved.

Consider the example of a blended family where life insurance trusts are used to benefit stepchildren equally. By designating life insurance proceeds to be distributed among stepchildren, the grantor ensures that these family members are provided for without impacting the inheritance of legacy children. This approach allows for a clear and equitable distribution that acknowledges the unique roles of each family member.

In another scenario, a family might establish trusts with staggered distributions to account for different life stages. This strategy ensures that beneficiaries receive support tailored to their specific needs, such as funding for education or housing at critical points in their lives.

Thoughtful planning will not only see to the immediate needs of beneficiaries – it also demonstrates the grantor's commitment to fairness and family harmony as the years go by and family needs change. Having a plan in place, such as a well-organized trust, will make it so much easier to adjust for changes that will surely come.

Creating trusts for blended families involves balancing diverse needs and relationships while ensuring fairness and transparency. By leveraging tools such as proportional distributions, separate trusts, and marital agreements, you can navigate the complexities of blended family dynamics and provide for all members in a way that honors their unique contributions and relationships

This concludes Chapter Nine.

To summarize, we emphasized the importance of meeting the financial needs and stability of each heir and fairly rewarding members who are contributing more to the estate. We mentioned the role of Discretionary Trusts in preparing for unpredictable events. The challenge of conflicting interests among siblings and managing expectations across multiple generations will require strategies for addressing conflicts such as mediation and family meetings – even more so with blended families.

In the next chapter, you will learn ways to help family members overcome fear and anxiety related to misconceptions about trusts.

Taking time now to choose the right trust will make a huge difference for your heirs...

CHAPTER 10
COMING TO PEACE WITH YOUR BEST TRUST

Recent surveys indicate a likelihood that 30% of Americans may have a will in place. Around 40% explain they simply haven't gotten around to it. Many believe they just don't have enough assets to leave to someone, so why bother? Some estimates suggest around 18% of Americans who actually have an estate plan have elected to build a trust.

Consider the story of a small business owner, Mark, who spent years building a successful enterprise. As he started to take serious steps with his estate planning, the idea of setting up a trust filled him with apprehension. He feared losing control over his assets. He worried about potential family disputes. He was overwhelmed by his nagging perception that trust management was just too complex. Mark got busy and never took action to learn more. Mark also put off his estate planning until, one day, life took a surprise turn. His unexpected demise left his grieving family to pick up the pieces. He did have a will, but it had not been updated in several years.

Mark is not alone. Many people experience similar anxieties when they think about the idea of setting up a trust. This is an irrational fear. As you may already know, fear can paralyze decision-making. This causes unreasonable delay.

Ultimately, no decision becomes a default decision – and time tricks the procrastinator, gradually inching him into a corner from where he cannot escape because he runs out of options. Trapped by his own anxieties and failure to decide, he fails to realize he is jeopardizing his financial legacy – as well as the welfare of his family.

10.1 FACE THE FACTS – FACE YOUR FEAR

One of the most common fears associated with trusts is the perceived loss of control over assets. Many people worry that transferring their hard-earned wealth into a trust means relinquishing their ability to manage it. However, understanding the structure and purpose of trusts can help alleviate this fear. Revocable trusts, for example, allow you to retain control and make changes as needed.

Another significant concern is the potential for family disputes. Individuals often fear that setting up a trust might lead to conflicts among heirs. This worry is rooted in the misconception that trusts complicate the inheritance process. In reality, a well-structured trust can prevent disputes by clearly outlining asset distribution.

The complexity of trust management is another source of anxiety. The legal jargon and financial intricacies can seem daunting, especially for those unfamiliar with estate planning. However, procrastination in setting up a trust can have serious consequences. Delaying planning can lead to increased emotional stress, as the uncertainty surrounding asset protection and distribution weighs heavily on family relationships. It's crucial to address these fears head-on, acknowledging that they are natural but not insurmountable. Families can face these challenges together, using open communication and shared decision-making to build a trust that reflects everyone's needs and values.

To overcome trust-related anxieties, education and preparation are key. By seeking knowledge about how trusts operate, you can dispel myths and gain confidence in your decision-making. Educational resources, such as workshops, books, and online courses, will give you added insights into the benefits and mechanics of trusts.

Trusted advisors, including estate planning attorneys and financial advisors, can offer expert guidance and support. These professionals not only clarify legal terms but also provide reassurance, ensuring that your trust aligns with your goals and protects your assets effectively.

Consider a few examples of everyday people just like yourself who have successfully navigated their fear of trusts. One couple, initially hesitant about setting up a trust, found peace of mind through careful planning and expert advice. They reported a reduction in stress and a newfound confidence in their financial future.

Another individual, who initially viewed trusts as overwhelming, discovered the benefits of a revocable trust. By maintaining control over his assets, he was able to adapt his estate plan as circumstances changed. This gave him flexibility as well as security.

Reflection Section: Overcoming Trust Anxieties

Take a moment to reflect on your own feelings about trusts. Consider the following questions to help identify and address any anxieties:

- What specific aspects of trusts are causing you concern?
- How might gaining a better understanding of trusts alleviate these fears?
- Have you consulted with trusted advisors who can provide clarity and support?
- In what ways can involving your family in the trust planning process help address concerns and build consensus?

Acknowledge your own fears and address them with facts. Consult with qualified professional trust advisors. Bring family members into the discussion. Work to build a consensus. Together, you can approach trust planning with confidence and peace of mind.

10.2 COMMUNICATING WITH FAMILY ABOUT TRUSTS

Communication is the cornerstone of successful trust planning. The process of setting up a trust involves not just legalities but also the hopes and dreams you have for your family's future. Open dialogue with family members is vital to ensure transparency and understanding.

By discussing your intentions and the details of the trust, you align family expectations, reducing the risk of misunderstandings and conflicts. It sets a foundation where everyone is on the same page, which is particularly important when multiple beneficiaries are involved.

Misaligned expectations can lead to disputes, but clear communication can prevent these issues before they arise. It's about creating an environment where your family feels involved and informed, thus fostering trust and cooperation.

Starting these conversations might seem daunting, but approaching them with intention can make a huge difference. Choose a time and setting that encourages open discussion, free from distractions and pressures.

This might mean setting aside a quiet evening at home or arranging a family meeting on neutral ground.

Preparing key points and information beforehand will give you confidence and clarity. Be ready to explain the purpose of the trust, who the beneficiaries are, and how the assets will be managed. Lay out the reasons behind your decisions, and be open to questions and feedback. This preparation shows that you value their input and are committed to transparency.

Effective communication requires active listening. Active listening involves genuinely considering the concerns and questions your family members might have. Using clear, non-technical language is essential to help everyone understand the trust's terms and implications.

Avoid legal jargon that might confuse those unfamiliar with estate planning. Instead, present the information in a way that resonates with their everyday experiences. This approach encourages engagement and makes the discussion more relatable. It helps build rapport and ensures that everyone feels heard and respected, which is vital for achieving consensus.

There are numerous examples of families who have successfully navigated these discussions, leading to positive outcomes. One family found that by holding regular meetings, they could align on shared financial goals, creating a unified vision for their estate. This ongoing dialogue allowed them to make informed, collaborative decisions about the trust's terms, fostering a sense of ownership and commitment.

Another family faced initial resistance but used open communication to address concerns. By actively listening and adjusting the trust's terms to reflect the family's collective needs, they transformed potential conflict into a collaborative effort that strengthened their bonds. These stories illustrate the power of communication in trust planning, showing that with the right approach, you can build a trust that not only secures your assets but also unites your family.

10.3 EMOTIONAL CONSIDERATIONS IN TRUST PLANNING

When you embark on the process of trust planning, the emotional motivations behind your decisions often run deep, rooted in a moral obligation to care for and protect your family. This desire can be a powerful force, driving you to establish a trust as a means of providing for your dependents and ensuring their financial security.

Some may also view their best Trust as a way to extend their influence and values beyond their lifetime, offering a tangible connection to future generations. This intent to leave a lasting impact shapes the way they approach estate planning.

However, these emotional drivers can also introduce complexities into the trust planning process. Avoiding favoritism among heirs while trying to be fair to everyone can be challenging. You may feel torn between wanting to treat all beneficiaries equally and recognizing the individual needs or contributions of each. This can be particularly difficult if there have been past conflicts or if family dynamics are intricate.

Beware of emotions that cloud judgment and lead to decisions that compromise you're your best intentions. Sensitivity and a willingness to confront difficult conversations will help you build your best Trust, one that complies with your best intentions and preserves your values.

Addressing emotional challenges effectively may mean you need to consider engaging a family mediator. A mediator can facilitate discussions, helping to resolve tensions and ensure that all voices are heard. This third-party perspective can be invaluable in maintaining objectivity and finding solutions that honor family relationships while achieving your goals.

Incorporating family values into the trust's objectives is another strategy. By clearly articulating these values, you can create a framework that guides decision-making and shapes the trust's terms. This might involve setting priorities that reflect shared beliefs or establishing conditions that promote responsible stewardship of the assets.

There are numerous instances where emotionally informed trust planning has led to successful outcomes. Consider a family that prioritized education as a core value. Their trust included provisions for funding higher education, ensuring that future generations could pursue their dreams without financial barriers. This decision not only provided practical support but also reinforced the importance of learning as a family tradition.

In another example, a trust was designed to honor a beloved family member's legacy by supporting charitable causes they were passionate about. This approach preserved the individual's memory while fostering a sense of continuity and purpose among the heirs.

Ultimately, trust planning is as much about the heart as it is about finances. By acknowledging and addressing the emotional dimensions involved, you can create a trust that not only secures assets but also strengthens family bonds and honors the legacy you wish to leave.

10.4 SEEK PROFESSIONAL ADVICE: BUILD CONFIDENCE WITH KNOWLEDGE

The cornerstone of effective trust planning is knowledge. Understanding the legal foundations of trusts empowers you to create a trust that aligns with your objectives and caters to your family's unique needs.

Many people mistakenly believe trusts are only for the wealthy, but the truth is, they're accessible to anyone keen on safeguarding their assets and ensuring a smooth transfer of wealth. Grasping the intricacies of how trusts work eliminates uncertainty and anxiety, replacing them with confidence and clarity.

A well-structured trust acts as a financial safety net, allowing you to prepare for the future with certainty. It's not just a document; it's a comprehensive plan for your family's security and cohesion, facilitating unity and trust.

Building confidence in trust decisions involves actively engaging your family in the planning process. By involving them, you lay a foundation of transparency and trust that can extend across generations. Set regular dates to review and update trust documents, ensuring they reflect current circumstances and future goals.

Transparency is pivotal; maintaining open communication with all stakeholders fosters an environment where everyone feels included and informed. This approach not only strengthens familial bonds but also ensures that the trust evolves with your family's changing needs. It reinforces the idea that estate planning is a collaborative effort, one that benefits from diverse perspectives and shared aspirations.

Professional support plays a crucial role in bolstering your confidence during the trust planning process.

Advisors offer expert insights, providing reassurance that your trust is structured to meet both legal requirements and personal goals. Their ongoing support and advice help navigate complex decisions, ensuring that you remain informed and empowered.

Reputable qualified professionals act as guides, simplifying the intricate details and offering solutions tailored to your situation. By leveraging their expertise, you gain a deeper understanding of the potential and flexibility trusts offer, enabling you to make decisions grounded in knowledge and foresight.

Take, for example, a family that holds regular follow-up meetings with their advisors. This consistent engagement ensures that their estate plan remains relevant and effective, adapting to life changes and new legal developments. These meetings provide a platform for discussing any concerns or adjustments, allowing the family to approach trust management proactively.

Another successful strategy involves organizing family workshops to educate and engage all members. These workshops serve as a space for learning and collaboration, where family members can ask questions and express concerns. The end result will be a clearer understanding of the trust's purpose and benefits. This educational approach demystifies the trust process and fosters a sense of ownership and confidence.

A trust is more than cold legalities. It is a comprehensive plan to perpetuate time-honored traditions, family connections, support dependents, and instill principles of industry, thrift, self-reliance, and service to others.

This concludes Chapter Ten.

To summarize, we talked about the importance of getting the facts and facing your fears, the need to communicate – especially with family members who will become parties to your Trust. We also discussed the value of respecting emotional realities and the benefits that will come from seeking professional advice. Let knowledge replace your fears; build your future with confidence.

The next chapter leads you in an exploration of how to plan for the long term.

CHAPTER 11
LONG-TERM TRUST PLANNING AND FUTURE PROOFING

Imagine waking up one day to find that the carefully crafted trust you set up to secure your family's future no longer aligns with your current life situation. Such is the dynamic nature of life. You must be ready to adapt to change. Your trust is adaptable. Trusts are not static documents; they are living entities designed to be flexible and evolve to accommodate significant milestones and shifts in personal circumstances.

As life unfolds, events such as marriage, birth or adoption, a sudden turn in health or death of a family member, or a significant change in wealth will necessitate revisiting and modifying your trust. Understanding when and how to make these adjustments is crucial for maintaining a trust that reflects your current intentions and family structure.

11.1 ADAPTING TRUSTS FOR LIFE CHANGES

Marriage or divorce profoundly impacts trust arrangements. Trust grantors will normally need to add your spouse as a beneficiary and make changes to the trust that reflect new joint financial goals.

In the case of divorce, removal of a former spouse from the trust or reassigning assets may become necessary to protect the grantor's interests.

Courts scrutinize the origins of assets and the intention behind their inclusion in a trust, making it vital to understand how these changes affect your estate plan. Such events necessitate a thorough review of your trust to understand what changes are necessary with your current marital status and financial commitments.

The joyous arrival of a child or the adoption of a new family member also calls for trust modifications. These changes often lead to a reevaluation of beneficiary designations and distribution schedules. Setting aside specific assets for your new child's education or future needs may require detailed amendments to your trust.

Similarly, significant changes in wealth or income demand attention. Whether through inheritance, a successful business venture, or other financial windfalls, it might be advantageous for you to transfer your new assets into your trust.

Updating your trust in response to life changes involves a structured process. You need to begin by consulting with legal and financial advisors. These professionals will help you make sure all your amendments to your Trust will comply with legal standards and align with your financial objectives.

Next, be sure to document all changes clearly. Amendments to your Trust will need to be executed legally with formal documentation and, in some cases, the additional witness of a notary public. This step not only protects your interests but also provides clarity for trustees and beneficiaries, reducing the potential for future disputes or misunderstandings.

Life changes significantly impact trust beneficiaries. A new marriage might introduce additional beneficiaries, such as stepchildren, necessitating adjustments in distribution schedules. Conversely, a divorce could lead to the removal of beneficiaries, reflecting the new family dynamics. These changes require careful consideration to ensure that all parties' needs and expectations are balanced. The addition of children may prompt a shift in asset allocation, redirecting funds to support their upbringing and education.

Consider the case of a business owner who experienced a substantial financial gain after selling a company. This windfall necessitated a reevaluation of his trust, incorporating provisions for his new spouse and adjusting asset allocations to reflect his increased wealth. By consulting with advisors and updating the trust, he ensured that his financial legacy aligned with his current life stage and aspirations.

Another example involves a family who adopted a child, prompting a comprehensive review of their trust to include the child's future needs. By revisiting their estate plan, they secured their child's financial future, ensuring that their intentions were clearly documented and executed.

Reflection Section: Assessing Your Trust's Adaptability

- Identify Life Changes: Reflect on recent life events that may require trust updates.
- Consult Professionals: Have you engaged with legal and financial advisors to guide modifications?
- Document Changes: Ensure all amendments are clearly documented and legally executed.
- Review Beneficiary Impact: Consider how changes affect beneficiary designations and distributions.

11.2 FUTURE-PROOFING YOUR TRUST AGAINST LEGISLATIVE CHANGES

In the ever-evolving landscape of tax and estate planning laws, staying informed is not just beneficial—it's crucial. Legislative changes can significantly impact how trusts are taxed and managed, potentially altering the effectiveness of your estate plan. New tax laws, for instance, can affect the tax implications of your trust, influencing how much of your estate is ultimately passed on to your beneficiaries.

Changes in estate planning regulations might introduce new requirements or opportunities that could either challenge or benefit your current arrangements. If you ignore these things, you could miss strategic opportunities for increasing your wealth; worse, you may suffer unintended financial consequences. It becomes important to keep abreast of these changes. You will want to make sure your trust remains compliant and effective.

To navigate these legislative changes, regular consultations with estate planning professionals are invaluable. These experts are well-versed in the latest legal developments and can provide insights on how changes might affect your trust. They can help you understand complex legislative language and identify which aspects of your trust may need adjustment.

Additionally, incorporating flexible terms into your trust documents can preemptively accommodate potential legal shifts. For instance, including provisions that allow for the adjustment of distribution schedules or the reallocation of assets can ensure that your trust remains adaptable, no matter how the legal landscape changes. This proactive approach minimizes disruptions and maintains the integrity of your estate planning.

Legal advisors play a pivotal role in future-proofing trusts. They can anticipate legislative changes and provide timely updates on relevant developments. This foresight allows you to make informed decisions and adjust your trust accordingly before changes take effect. Advisors can recommend specific amendments or strategies that align your trust with new laws, ensuring compliance and maximizing benefits. For example, if new legislation reduces estate tax thresholds, an advisor might suggest adjustments to your trust's asset allocation to mitigate potential tax liabilities. By leveraging their expertise, you can navigate the complexities of changing laws with confidence and precision.

Consider the implications of a legislative shift that adjusts estate tax thresholds. In such cases, trusts may need to be modified to optimize tax efficiency and ensure compliance. For instance, if the exemption threshold decreases, more estates could become subject to taxation, prompting the need for strategic adjustments to minimize tax exposure. Similarly, changes in beneficiary rights laws might necessitate revisions to trust documents to reflect updated legal standards. An instance of this could be a new law expanding the rights of beneficiaries, requiring trusts to include additional provisions or clarifications. These examples highlight the importance of staying informed and proactive, ensuring that your trust remains aligned with evolving legal requirements.

Reflection Section: Staying Ahead of Legislative Changes

- Monitor Legal Developments: Regularly check for updates in tax and estate planning laws.
- Consultation Cadence: Schedule regular meetings with legal advisors to discuss potential impacts.
- Flexibility in Terms: Review your trust's terms to ensure adaptability to legal changes.
- Proactive Adjustments: Consider preemptive modifications to align with anticipated legislative shifts.

By actively engaging with these strategies, you ensure that your trust remains robust and resilient, ready to weather any legislative changes that come its way.

11.3 DYNASTY TRUSTS: PLANNING FOR GENERATIONAL WEALTH

Dynasty trusts are a unique and strategic estate planning tool designed to preserve wealth across multiple generations. Unlike typical trusts that might have a set termination date, dynasty trusts are created to last in perpetuity, allowing assets to be passed down through the family for generations without the burden of estate taxes. At the heart of a dynasty trust is the idea of intergenerational wealth transfer. This means the trust assets can continue to grow and benefit family members long into the future.

One significant advantage is the avoidance of generation-skipping transfer taxes, which typically apply when wealth is passed directly to a grandchild rather than a child. By utilizing a dynasty trust, you can ensure that your financial legacy endures, providing for your descendants while minimizing tax liabilities.

Strategically, dynasty trusts serve as a pillar for long-term family financial goals. They are particularly effective for providing for the educational expenses of future generations, ensuring that your descendants have the resources to pursue higher education without financial strain. This can be a transformative gift, empowering your family to achieve academic and professional success without the weight of student debt.

Additionally, dynasty trusts can maintain family businesses within the trust, securing the business's future and keeping it within the family. By holding the business interests in a trust, you can establish governance structures and succession plans that ensure the business remains aligned with your family's values and vision.

Establishing a dynasty trust requires careful consideration of legal and administrative requirements. One critical step is choosing a jurisdiction with favorable laws for perpetual trusts. Not all states allow trusts to exist indefinitely, so selecting a state with flexible or abolished rule against perpetuities is essential. This ensures that the trust can legally operate for generations.

Appointing trustees with a long-term commitment is equally important. Trustees will manage the trust's assets and ensure that your intentions are honored over time. Selecting individuals or institutions that understand your family's goals and have the expertise to manage complex estates is crucial for the trust's success. Trustees must be capable of navigating changing financial landscapes and adapting strategies to preserve and grow the trust's assets.

The success of dynasty trusts is evident in real-world examples. Consider the Rockefeller family, whose dynasty trust has maintained and grown their wealth for over a century. The trust not only supports the family's financial needs but also funds philanthropic endeavors, impacting global public health, education, and environmental conservation. This trust exemplifies how strategic planning and thoughtful management can sustain wealth and values across generations.

Another example might involve a family that establishes a dynasty trust to support educational scholarships and community projects, ensuring that their legacy positively influences society. Through careful planning and execution, dynasty trusts can provide both financial security and a lasting legacy, demonstrating their potential to transform family wealth into a force for good across generations.

11.4 REVIEWING AND UPDATING TRUSTS REGULARLY

Trusts are not meant to be set and forgotten. They require regular attention to ensure they continue to meet your needs and reflect your current life situation. Periodic reviews are vital because life evolves, and so do your financial circumstances and family dynamics. Over time, certain provisions in your trust might become outdated or irrelevant, no longer aligning with your objectives.

Perhaps you've experienced a significant shift in your financial landscape, such as an increase or decrease in wealth. These changes might necessitate adjustments in how assets are managed or distributed to beneficiaries. Recognizing and addressing these outdated elements ensures that your trust remains a dynamic tool, fully aligned with your current goals and needs.

Conducting a thorough trust review involves a systematic approach. Begin by examining beneficiary designations. Are the right individuals or entities still listed, or do changes in your family structure warrant updates? This step is crucial to ensure that your assets are distributed according to your latest intentions.

Next, assess trustee appointments. Trustees play a pivotal role in managing your trust, so it's important to ensure that those appointed are still willing and capable of fulfilling their responsibilities. Evaluating the performance of trust investments is also essential. Are the assets performing as expected, or do they require reallocation to better suit your financial strategy? Regular reviews of these components help maintain the trust's effectiveness and relevance.

Professional advisors can be invaluable allies during these reviews. Legal and financial experts offer insights into best practices, identifying areas for enhancement and ensuring compliance with current legal standards. They can pinpoint potential improvements, such as integrating tax-efficient strategies or optimizing asset allocations to enhance trust performance.

Advisors also provide a fresh perspective, helping you see beyond your immediate concerns and consider long-term implications. Their expertise ensures that your trust remains a robust and compliant vehicle for achieving your estate planning goals, adapting to shifts in the legal landscape and your personal circumstances.

Consider the case of a family who, during a routine trust review, discovered that their trust terms were no longer aligned with new tax strategies. With guidance from their financial advisor, they updated their trust to take advantage of recent tax law changes, resulting in significant tax savings.

Another scenario involved a couple who regularly updated their trust to include new family beneficiaries, such as grandchildren, ensuring that their expanding family remained well-provided for.

These examples highlight the tangible benefits of regular trust reviews, demonstrating how proactive management can lead to improved outcomes and peace of mind.

Checklist for Trust Reviews:

- Beneficiary Designations: Confirm that listed beneficiaries reflect your current intentions.

- Trustee Appointments: Ensure trustees are still appropriate and capable of managing the trust.

- Investment Performance: Evaluate whether trust assets are generating expected returns.

- Legal Compliance: Verify that the trust adheres to current laws and best practices.

By staying proactive and engaging with professional advisors, you ensure that your trust remains an effective tool for managing and preserving your legacy.

This concludes Chapter Eleven. To summarize, we talked about strategies for adapting your Trust to changes in the lives of your beneficiaries, how to respond to changes in Trust laws, the benefits of a Dynasty Trust that makes it possible to pass your estate to multiple generations, and the importance of reviewing and updating your Trust on a regular basis.

Next, we will examine how to leverage technology to manage your trust.

CHAPTER 12
TOOLS, RESOURCES, AND FURTHER LEARNING

Imagine you're trying to solve a complex puzzle, each piece representing an aspect of managing a trust. Now, picture having a toolkit filled with the latest gadgets to help you fit those pieces together perfectly. This is the essence of leveraging technology in trust management today. With the right tools, you can streamline processes, enhance efficiency, and ensure security, turning what might seem like a daunting task into a manageable, even enjoyable, endeavor.

12.1 ESSENTIAL TOOLS FOR TRUST MANAGEMENT

In our increasingly digital world, technology offers remarkable solutions for trust management. For instance, accounting software like Quicken and QuickBooks can simplify financial tracking. These programs are designed to handle the intricacies of trust finances, offering features that help track income, expenses, and investments with precision. They allow you to generate detailed reports, ensuring transparency and accuracy in financial management. With these tools, you can maintain a clear understanding of your trust's financial health, making it easier to plan distributions and manage assets effectively.

Document management is so much more effective with technology. Systems that organize trust paperwork efficiently are invaluable. They allow you to store, retrieve, and manage documents with ease, ensuring that important legal papers and records are always accessible.

This is where platforms like "Estateably" come into play, offering robust solutions for document automation and management. With such systems, you can automate the generation of necessary forms, reducing the time spent on manual paperwork and minimizing errors. This not only enhances productivity but also ensures compliance with legal requirements, making trust administration smoother and more efficient.

Communication within trust management cannot be overstated. Maintaining secure and private communication with trustees and beneficiaries is paramount. Encrypted email services provide the confidentiality needed to discuss sensitive information without the risk of interception.

Additionally, secure file-sharing platforms, such as Dropbox or Google Drive with enhanced security settings, allow for the safe exchange of documents and information. These tools ensure that your communications remain private and protected, fostering trust and clarity among all parties involved.

Tracking and analyzing investments is crucial for maintaining the financial health of a trust. Portfolio management tools like Morningstar and Personal Capital offer comprehensive solutions for monitoring trust investments. These tools provide insights into performance, risk levels, and market trends, enabling you to make informed decisions about asset allocation and investment strategies. By leveraging these platforms, you can ensure that your trust's portfolio remains aligned with your financial goals, adapting to changes in the market as needed.

Efficiency in trust management is further enhanced by task management software and calendaring tools. Programs such as Asana or Trello help organize tasks, set reminders, and track progress, ensuring that nothing falls through the cracks. Calendaring tools like Google Calendar or Outlook can be used to schedule important deadlines and meetings, keeping you and your team on track. These tools not only improve organization but also enhance productivity, allowing you to manage trust-related tasks with greater ease and effectiveness.

Interactive Element: Trust Management Toolkit Checklist

Create a checklist of essential tools for trust management. Use this checklist to assess your current toolkit and identify areas for improvement. Consider which tools could enhance your efficiency and security, and prioritize their integration into your trust management routine.

Toolkit Checklist Categories you might consider:

___ Accounting Software

___ Document Management Systems

___ Secure Communication Tools

___ Investment Tracking Platforms

12.2 ON-LINE RESOURCES AND CONTINUING EDUCATION

The internet is a treasure trove of information, particularly when it comes to understanding and managing trusts. Finding reputable websites and online platforms is crucial for accessing reliable insights into trust management.

Estate planning blogs and websites like those featured in the "60 Best Estate Planning Blogs and Websites in 2025" offer a wealth of knowledge. These platforms provide updates on trust law, practical advice, and case studies that illuminate various aspects of estate planning.

Government resources on trust law and taxation are also invaluable. Websites run by tax authorities and legal bodies often provide free, authoritative information that can help demystify the complexities of trusts and estate laws. They offer official guidelines, updates on legislative changes, and tools to help you understand how these might affect your trust plans.

The role of online courses and webinars in enhancing trust knowledge cannot be overlooked. These digital platforms offer structured learning opportunities that can deepen your understanding of trust management. Continuing legal education (CLE) courses are particularly beneficial for those acting as trustees or those involved in the legal aspects of estate planning.

These courses cover a wide range of topics, including the latest changes in trust legislation, strategies for effective trust management, and ethical considerations. Webinars, on the other hand, provide more flexible learning options, often focusing on current trends in trust management. They are usually shorter and more interactive, allowing you to engage with experts in real-time and ask questions pertinent to your situation. Both formats are excellent for keeping up-to-date with the evolving landscape of trust and estate management.

Engaging with online forums and communities offers another layer of support and knowledge. These platforms allow you to connect with peers, share experiences, and seek advice in a supportive environment. Estate planning forums are particularly useful for peer support, where individuals share their challenges and solutions related to trust management. Such interactions can provide new perspectives and creative solutions to complex problems.

Professional network groups on platforms like LinkedIn can also be valuable. These groups often include trust and estate professionals who share insights, articles, and news relevant to trust management. Being part of these communities not only enhances your knowledge but also helps you build a network of contacts who can offer support and guidance.

You will be encouraged by the number of people just like you who have expanded their trust knowledge through online resources, illustrating the tangible benefits of these platforms. Many have reported significant professional development through online courses. These individuals often find themselves better equipped to handle the intricacies of trust management, having gained knowledge and confidence from structured learning environments.

Participants in virtual workshops often highlight the value of interactive learning. They learn directly from experts and gain insights from other participants just like them. The online platforms foster deeper understanding and greater confidence with the application of trust-related principles. The potential of online learning to transform your approach to trust management is rich and diverse. It will open access to tools and insights needed to navigate the legal field of trusts effectively.

12.3 BUILDING A NETWORK OF FINANCIAL AND LEGAL EXPERTS

In the realm of trust management, the value of networking with financial and legal experts cannot be overstated. Establishing a robust network of professionals provides you with access to specialized knowledge and advice that can significantly enhance your trust management strategies.

Experts in the field bring a wealth of experience and insights, helping you navigate complex legal and financial landscapes. This collaborative problem-solving approach ensures that you are not alone in making critical decisions, as you can rely on the shared expertise of your network to devise innovative solutions tailored to your unique circumstances. By fostering these connections, you create a support system that can offer guidance, answer questions, and provide reassurance as you manage your trust affairs.

Building such a network begins with strategically positioning yourself to meet the right people. Attending industry conferences and seminars is an excellent way to start. These events attract professionals from all over, providing a platform to engage with thought leaders, learn about the latest trends, and share experiences.

Conversations at these gatherings often lead to meaningful connections that can enrich your understanding of trust management.

Additionally, joining professional associations related to estate planning is another effective strategy. Membership in these organizations often grants access to exclusive resources, educational materials, and networking events. These associations offer a sense of community, where members can engage in discussions, seek advice, and collaborate on initiatives. By immersing yourself in these professional circles, you position yourself to build a network of contacts who can offer both immediate and long-term benefits.

Maintaining and nurturing these relationships is crucial for ensuring they remain beneficial over time. Regular communication and updates help keep the lines of interaction open, reinforcing the sense of partnership and collaboration. Sharing insights, challenges, and successes with your network not only strengthens these bonds but also fosters an environment of mutual support.

Offering referrals and acknowledging the contributions of others can further cement your standing within your network, as these acts demonstrate your commitment to the community. By cultivating these professional relationships, you create a dynamic network that evolves with your needs and continues to provide value as your trust management requirements change.

The impact of successful networking is huge in trust management. A financial advisor might collaborate with an attorney to structure a trust that optimizes tax benefits while ensuring compliance with legal standards. This collaboration could result in a tailored trust plan that addresses both financial and legal considerations, offering a comprehensive solution for the client. Accounts of individuals who have leveraged their networks for trust solutions points out the critical impact these relationships can have. Anyone facing a complex estate planning challenges will be relieved when connecting with experts who provided the necessary guidance to resolve the issue efficiently. This is the power of networking. A robust network will put you back in the driver's seat.

Building a network of financial and legal experts is not just about having names on a contact list; it's about creating a community of professionals who understand your goals and are invested in your success. By actively engaging with these experts, you gain access to a wealth of knowledge and resources that can enhance your trust management capabilities. As you continue to develop and nurture these relationships, you will be rewarded by the collaborative ecosystem that benefits both you and your network. You will be amazed by your opportunities for growth, learning, and success in managing your trust.

12.4 LEVERAGING TECHNOLOGY IN TRUST MANAGEMENT

In the ever-evolving landscape of trust management, technology stands as a transformative force, reshaping how we handle estates and assets. Consider the impact of artificial intelligence (AI), which offers predictive financial analysis tools that can forecast market trends and optimize investment strategies. These AI systems analyze vast amounts of data to provide insights that were once the realm of seasoned analysts, allowing trustees to make informed decisions with a level of precision and foresight previously unattainable. Imagine being able to predict potential financial shifts and adjust your trust's portfolio accordingly, ensuring that assets are not only protected but also positioned for growth. This use of AI turns data into actionable intelligence, offering a strategic advantage in trust administration.

Blockchain technology is another groundbreaking advancement, bringing unparalleled security to record-keeping. Its decentralized, immutable ledger ensures that all transactions and modifications are recorded with precision and transparency, reducing the risk of fraud and errors. This technology offers a secure and efficient way to manage trust documents, providing a clear and unalterable history of all actions taken.

The use of blockchain can streamline audits and compliance checks, offering peace of mind to trustees and beneficiaries alike. By integrating blockchain into trust management, you create a system where trust records are not only secure but also easily verifiable, enhancing accountability and reducing the potential for disputes.

Digital platforms significantly streamline trust management processes, making them more efficient and user-friendly. Online portals for beneficiary communication allow for seamless and secure interactions, ensuring that all parties are informed and engaged. These platforms provide a centralized location for sharing updates, distributing documents, and addressing inquiries, fostering transparency and collaboration.

Automated reporting and compliance tools further enhance efficiency by simplifying the generation of financial reports and ensuring adherence to regulatory requirements. These tools minimize the administrative burden on trustees, freeing up time and resources to focus on strategic decision-making and asset management.

Even with all the promising benefits of new technology, the good things do not come without opposition and challenges. A major concern is data security and privacy. As trust management increasingly relies on digital tools, safeguarding sensitive information becomes paramount. Implementing robust cybersecurity measures, such as encryption and multi-factor authentication, can protect data from unauthorized access.

Additionally, training for trustees and beneficiaries on the use of these new tools is essential. Providing comprehensive training sessions can help users understand the features and benefits of the technology, ensuring they use it effectively and confidently. This training also helps mitigate resistance to change, making the transition to tech-enhanced trust management smoother and more successful.

Many today have opted to use AI for investment strategies. The AI system analyzed historical data and current market conditions, offering recommendations that led to a diversified and resilient portfolio. This strategic shift not only protected assets during market downturns but also capitalized on growth opportunities, increasing the trust's overall value.

In another example, a trust utilized blockchain for record-keeping, significantly reducing the time and effort required for audits. The clear, tamper-proof records provided by blockchain technology ensured that all transactions were accurately documented, bolstering trust among all parties involved.

In this final chapter, we have talked about the profound impact technology can have on trust management. By embracing these advancements, you can enhance the efficiency, security, and effectiveness of your trust administration, ensuring that your assets are managed in a way that aligns with your goals and priorities.

As we look ahead, integrating technology into trust management not only addresses current challenges but also positions you to adapt to future developments and opportunities.

This concludes the final chapter. To summarize, we talked about online tools, platforms, and software you will want to consider in managing your Trust. We also discussed online resources for continuing your education about trusts, and emphasized the importance of building a network of experts, and recommended you use all these resources to leverage technology to manage your Trust.

We now come to the Conclusion. Before you read that, please turn this page for one final request.

As you hurry to finish reading, don't forget to plan a deep dive into the References and Resources provided at the end of this book.

Congratulations!

You are nearly finished!

I am excited you decided to read this book.

I sincerely hope you have enjoyed your read!
Will you consider leaving a review?

Most people will choose books based on reviews.

With your help, this book can reach many people just like you who may be undecided, real people who just need to see your kind words of reassurance.

To Post a Review

Open this link and sign into your Amazon account:

*https://Amazon.com/review/create-review?&asin=*0999745255

OR

Scan this QR Code, and sign into your account.

- Benjamin Carter

PS. See you at the end of your read! If you want, you may include a selfie holding this book with your review.

CONCLUSION

The topic of trusts can be complicated and confusing. Now that you are nearly finished reading this book, do you feel more confident? As a quick review, you have finished reading the following chapter topics:

1. Understanding Trusts
2. Choosing the Right Trust
3. Legal Framework and Trust Law
4. Finding the Right Professional Help
5. Funding Your Trust
6. Trust Management and Responsibilities
7. Tax Strategies and Implications
8. Protecting Assets with Trusts
9. Equitable Distribution Strategies
10. Coming to Peace with Your Best Trust
11. Long-Term Trust Planning and Future-Proofing
12. Tools, Resources, and Further Learning

i. SUMMARY

This has been a pointed discussion about the intricate world of trusts. The goal was to take the mystery out of trusts and their complexities, and highlight their vital role in estate planning.

Taking the long view today will help you be better prepared when that far off future arrives sooner than you expect, and reality suddenly looms before you.

A trust is a powerful tool that can safeguard your legacy and provide peace of mind for you and your loved ones.

Your best Trust will protect your assets, reduce taxes, and transfer generational wealth to your heirs.

Our discussion about the basic legal framework of trusts can help you as you talk with your trust advisors and work with your trustee. Let your professional team help with your final selection for a trustee.

Building the best trust for you will require extensive study, communication with family members, and collaboration with trust attorneys and qualified estate planning professionals.

You will need to review the information in this book as you search the references provided in the back to find the right professional help.

ii. KEY TAKE AWAYS

As you reflect on what you've learned, remember these key takeaways:

A simple will may not be enough to ensure your assets are fairly distributed to your heirs as you intend. To make sure this happens, you should consider a trust.

Trusts are not solely for the wealthy; they are versatile instruments that can benefit anyone looking to protect their financial future.

You now have the power to navigate the complexities of trusts with confidence. The knowledge you have gained from this book will empower you to secure your financial legacy.

Choosing the right trust requires careful consideration of your unique circumstances and goals.

Understanding the legal framework and tax implications can maximize the advantages trusts offer. Trusts can help your heirs avoid probate. Your best trust can provide for your dependents and also help shield your assets from unexpected claims upon your estate.

Trusts offer control and flexibility, allowing you to make informed decisions that align with your values and objectives.

iii. CALL TO ACTION

Now is the time to take action. Don't wait for some unscheduled tomorrow. If you can, start today. Check out the Action Item checklist provided right after this.

These steps are essential. You want to make sure your intentions are clearly documented and leave nothing to chance. You want to be certain the right legally binding tools are in place so someone you trust will see that your assets are distributed according to your wishes.

Take a moment to review your current financial situation and sincerely consider how a trust could enhance your estate plan. Consult with a qualified trust attorney to tailor a plan that meets your specific needs.

Find a good CPA or tax advisor who can assist you with tax strategies and equitable distribution plans. Engage with financial advisors who can help you manage and grow your assets effectively.

Don't get discouraged. Protecting your assets so your heirs can benefit from all your hard work is important.

Explore additional resources, attend workshops. Stay in touch with your financial advisor to keep yourself aware of changes in trust law and strategies. The landscape of estate planning is ever-evolving. Making a commitment to stay informed will help you keep your plans effective and relevant.

At the end of this book, you will find a wealth of references and links that will make your journey easier.

iv. CLOSING THOUGHT

Consider this:

"The best way to predict the future is to create it."

Turn the page to see a list of recommended Action Items.

Action Item List

1. Put time on your calendar to quietly think.
2. Consult this book to organize your thoughts – return to it frequently.
3. Research the references and resources listed at the end of this book.
4. Review your finances to evaluate how a trust could enhance your estate plan.
5. Write down your personal action plan, but make changes over time as needed.
6. Calendar key actions, but be flexible – and above all, don't give up.
7. Find a financial advisor you trust.
8. Consult with a qualified reputable trust attorney.
9. Discuss your trust with family members and others who will be parties to the trust.
10. Decide on the type of trust that best aligns with your goals and your family's needs.
11. Consider how you will fund your trust.
12. Work with your financial advisor to organize your assets.
13. Interview potential trustees. Decide who fits the role.
14. Ask your attorney to draft the trust documents.
15. Review your trust with your Trustee and your attorney.

16. Make sure your Trustee understands and agrees to shoulder this burden.
17. Make sure all your heirs have been fairly considered in each of their unique situations – especially vulnerable dependents with special needs.
18. Communicate with your family and any other parties to the trust.
19. Arrange for coordinating all required signatures.
20. Work with your Trustee and your attorney to schedule periodic reviews – to keep your trust up to date.
21. Congratulations – your best trust will then become a living reality.

Create your brighter future, Build your Best Trust

REFERENCES AND RESOURCES

#	**Titles and URL's**
1	*The Fundamentals of Trusts | The Princetone Sharpe Group* https://www.oppenheimer.com/sharpegroup/assets/pdf/the-fundamentals-of-trusts_tpsg.pdf
2	*10 Common Misconceptions About Trusts* https://www.yourlegacylegalcare.com/post/10-common-misconceptions-about-trusts
3	*Will vs. Trust: What Do You Need? Cost, Process and Uses* https://www.nerdwallet.com/article/investing/estate-planning/will-vs-trust#:~:text=The%20main%20difference%20between%20wills,typically%20must%20go%20through%20probate
4	*11 Pros and Cons of Charitable Remainder Trusts (CRTs)* https://www.reninc.com/charitable-remainder-trusts-pros-and-cons/
5	*Revocable Trust vs. Irrevocable Trust: What's the Difference?* https://www.investopedia.com/ask/answers/071615/what-difference-between-revocable-trust-and-living-trust.asp#:~:text=Revocable%2C%20or%20living%2C%20trusts%20can,that%20revocable%20trusts%20do%20not
6	*Understanding Living Trusts: Benefits & Key Myths Explained* https://bluenotary.us/living-trust/
7	*Testamentary Trust: Definition & How It Works* https://www.metlife.com/stories/legal/testamentary-trust/
8	*LII Wex special needs trust - Law.Cornell.Edu* https://www.law.cornell.edu/wex/special_needs_trust
9	*Uniform Trust Code*

	https://en.wikipedia.org/wiki/Uniform_Trust_Code
10	*fiduciary duties of trustees | Wex - Law.Cornell.Edu* https://www.law.cornell.edu/wex/fiduciary_duties_of_trustees
11	*Trusts and the Probate Process: What You Should Know* https://www.czepigalaw.com/blog/trusts-and-the-probate-process-what-you-should-know/
12	*Common Mistakes You Can Avoid When Creating a Trust* https://www.schomerlawgroup.com/trust/common-mistakes-you-can-avoid-when-creating-a-trust/
13	*Choose A Trust Lawyer: Qualities & Questions* https://amyharringtonlaw.com/choosing-a-trust-lawyer-key-qualities-and-questions-to-consider/
14	*Financial Advisor as a Trustee?* https://www.steffensfinancial.com/blog/financial-advisor-as-a-trustee
15	*Trusts Decoded: Simplifying Complex Legal Jargon* https://www.vancouverwillsandtrusts.com/blog/trusts-decoded-simplifying-complex-legal-jargon
16	*Trust Advisory Committees for Succession Planning* https://masource.org/education/articles/trust-advisory-committees-for-succession-planning/
17	*How to Transfer Property into a Trust* https://smartasset.com/estate-planning/how-to-transfer-property-into-a-trust
18	*The Role of Trusts in Asset Protection and Growth* https://www.snyderlawpc.com/the-role-of-trusts-in-asset-protection-and-growth/

19	*Federal income tax and trust strategies | Trusts and taxes* https://www.fidelity.com/viewpoints/wealth-management/insights/trusts-and-taxes
20	*Funding a Trust in 2024: A Comprehensive Guide to ...* https://www.gentreo.com/funding-a-trust-in-2023-a-comprehensive-guide-to-protecting-your-assets-and-legacy-2
21	*What Is a Trustee? Definition, Role, and Duties* https://www.investopedia.com/terms/t/trustee.asp
22	*Maximize Your Trust Fund: Strategies for High Net Worth ...* https://www.savvywealth.com/blog-posts/maximizing-your-trust-fund-strategies-for-high-net-worth-individuals-and-families-in-2024
23	*Helping Trustees Avoid Liability – The Duty of Record ...* https://www.faegredrinker.com/en/insights/publications/2019/7/helping-trustees-avoid-liability-the-duty-of-record-keeping-and-identification-of-trust-property
24	*Trust Amendment Form - How to Amend Your Trust | Trust & Will* https://trustandwill.com/learn/trust-amendment-form#:~:text=A%20Trust%20amendment%20form%20is%20used%20to%20make%20official%20updates,difficulties%20in%20court%20later%20on.
25	*A Short Primer on Trusts and Trust Taxation* https://www.specialneedsalliance.org/the-voice/a-short-primer-on-trusts-and-trust-taxation/
26	*Income Tax Implications of Grantor and Non-Grantor Trusts* https://www.claconnect.com/en/resources/articles/income-tax-implications-of-grantor-and-nongrantor-trusts
27	*Navigating Estate Tax Planning* https://www.texastrustlaw.com/navigating-estate-tax-planning/

28	*Trust & Estate Compliance Mastery* https://www.estateably.com/blog/mastering-compliance-reporting-in-trust-and-estate-administration
29	*Asset Protection Trusts: Guide to Benefits & Drawbacks* https://bluenotary.us/asset-protection-trust/
30	*Offshore vs. Domestic Trust for Legal Asset Protection* https://www.assetprotectionplanners.com/asset-protection-trust/offshore-vs-domestic-2/
31	*Asset protection trusts: strategies for estate planning* https://www.investmentnews.com/guides/asset-protection-trusts-strategies-for-estate-planning/252075
32	*Benefits of Trust Ownership for Businesses and Real Estate* https://stories.td.com/us/en/article/benefits-of-trust-ownership-for-businesses-and-real-estate
33	*Trust Management: How to Minimize Disputes & Family ...* https://www.privatebank.bankofamerica.com/articles/trust-administration-issues.html
34	*Discretionary trusts: 5 benefits and disadvantages* https://pooleadvisory.com.au/financial-advice/discretionary-trusts-5-benefits-and-disadvantages
35	*How to handle the emotions involved in trust planning* https://www.usbank.com/wealth-management/financial-perspectives/trust-and-estate-planning/trust-planning-handling-the-emotions-involved.html
36	*Estate Planning for Blended Families: The Role of Trusts* https://wealthcarelawyer.com/articles/trusts/estate-planning-for-blended-families-the-role-of-trusts/

37	*Why are people afraid of estate planning?* https://legacyassuranceplan.com/articles/why-plan/why-are-people-afraid-of-estate-planning
38	*Avoiding Family Feuds: Open Communication in Estate ...* https://beaconlegacygroup.com/avoiding-family-feuds-open-communication-in-estate-planning/
39	*Designing for Trust: The Crucial Role in Digital User ...* https://uxpajournal.org/designing-for-trust-the-crucial-role-in-digital-user-experiences/
40	*Trust: A Financial Advisor's Most Important Asset* https://www.investopedia.com/financial-advisor/trust-advisors-most-important-asset/
41	*Trust assets and divorce: How is equitable division determined?* https://legacyassuranceplan.com/articles/trusts/trust-assets-and-divorce-equitable-division-determined#:~:text=For%20trust%20assets%2C%20a%20prenuptial,be%20handled%20during%20a%20divorce.
42	*The Future of Estate Planning: Preparing for a New Wave ...* https://arizonastatelawjournal.org/2024/01/23/the-future-of-estate-planning-preparing-for-a-new-wave-of-laws-and-regulations/
43	*Successful Dynasty Trusts in History: The Rockefeller Family* https://www.mrclawcorp.com/blog/successful-dynasty-trusts-in-history-the-rockefeller-family/
44	*Trusts and Year-End Planning: A Checklist* https://www.elements.org/wealth/articles/2023/trusts-and-year-end-planning-a-checklist/
45	*Estateably: Estate and Trust Administration Software* https://www.estateably.com/

46	*60 Best Estate Planning Blogs and Websites in 2025* https://legal.feedspot.com/estate_planning_blogs/
47	*Networking Strategies for Financial Advisors in 2023* https://money.usnews.com/financial-advisors/articles/networking-strategies-for-financial-advisors-in-2023
48	*Artificial Intelligence (AI) and Trust and Estate Law* https://www.actec.org/resources-for-wealth-planning-professionals/artificial-intelligence-and-trust-and-estate-law-ai/

Benjamin Carter

Benjamin Carter is a pen name whose image and likeness portrayed above was derived using Artificial Intelligence. The author partners with Read and Learn Publishing as a new brand dedicated to creating enlightening articles and books that make knowledge and understanding accessible and engaging for everyday readers. The author brings a talent for writing, a passion for clarity and a commitment to simplicity. Whether it's estate planning and personal finance, travel or personal development, arts and crafts, gardening, model trains, sports, you name it, the author's compelling conversational style invites readers to learn without feeling overwhelmed. He also looks for opportunities to dig a little deeper and share details that help the reader understand the real underlying issues.

At Read and Learn Publishing, the goal is simple: making knowledge – and the personal power that comes with it – accessible to anyone.

Printed in Dunstable, United Kingdom

91342774R00111